T0265817

Creatures Are Stirring

A Guide to Architectural Companionship

Published by Applied Research and Design Publishing, an imprint of ORO Editions.
Gordon Goff: Publisher

www.appliedresearchanddesign.com
info@appliedresearchanddesign.com

Copyright © 2021 Joseph Altshuler and Julia Sedlock

All rights reserved. No part of this book may be reproduced, stored in a retrieval system, or transmitted in any form or by any means, including electronic, mechanical, photocopying of microfilming, recording, or otherwise (except that copying permitted by Sections 107 and 108 of the U.S. Copyright Law and except by reviewers for the public press) without written permission from the publisher.

You must not circulate this book in any other binding or cover and you must impose this same condition on any acquirer.

Authors: Joseph Altshuler and Julia Sedlock
Copyediting: Jayne Kelley
Book Design: Matthew Harlan
Illustrations: Zack Morrison and Joseph Altshuler (Could Be Architecture)
Project Manager: Jake Anderson

10 9 8 7 6 5 4 3 2 1 First Edition

ISBN: 978-1-951541-61-3

Color Separations and Printing: ORO Group Ltd.
Printed in China.

AR+D Publishing makes a continuous effort to minimize the overall carbon footprint of its publications. As part of this goal, AR+D, in association with Global ReLeaf, arranges to plant trees to replace those used in the manufacturing of the paper produced for its books. Global ReLeaf is an international campaign run by American Forests, one of the world's oldest nonprofit conservation organizations. Global ReLeaf is American Forests' education and action program that helps individuals, organizations, agencies, and corporations improve the local and global environment by planting and caring for trees.

Creatures Are Stirring

A Guide to Architectural Companionship

JOSEPH ALTSHULER
JULIA SEDLOCK

APPLIED
RESEARCH
+DESIGN
PUBLISHING

TABLE OF CONTENTS

FOREWORD

WORLD OF RELATIVES

A critical component of Indigenous ontology is the notion of relationality—that is, the concept that all living things are related. That relation is familial, and we have responsibility to foster and be good stewards of those relationships. I believe we should be thinking about architecture as our relations. Buildings are characters and actors within the living world. They breathe, sweat, and produce waste. I am trying to expand the notion of how architecture can be thought of as living actors in our world. To me, this includes the modalities we use to represent our designed relatives.

—**Chris T. Cornelius (Oneida)**, designer and educator, Milwaukee

WORLD OF WINDOW SHOPPING

I'm walking with my feet dipped in the river, the water caressing my toes. From my height, I feel like the female Goliath. I'm on the hunt for a dress. Chicago is the best department store to find one, carrying fashionable pieces from Sullivan and Lloyd Wright to Mies and Goldberg. I am immediately drawn to the Marina City towers. I put my legs in, pulling the marina up and squeezing myself to fit. The concrete softens on my body, turning the tower into a silk dress. It is tailored perfectly—a custom garment embroidered with sequined balconies. I'm beaming like a lighthouse above the city and lake, my hands resting on my hips. With the CNA Building lipstick and the Stock Exchange arch necklace, my outfit is complete. Chicago is my wardrobe, my playground, and my intimate inspiration.

—**Nelly Agassi,** artist and educator, Chicago

WORLD OF WORDS

I sit cross-legged and eyes closed, still. It's in this quiet space where many of my worlds agreed to meet. My first true friends were words. Words and worlds, first cousins, maybe even siblings, or lovers, come together to create. In such a vast ecosystem, I'm so blessed that words chose me as a companion.

—**Roy Kinsey**, rapper and librarian, Chicago

WORLD OF MEMES

Imagine a world where solidarity between humans is the best it has ever been. Imagine a world where we people loved other human beings more than our pets. Imagine if we cared about abolition in the same way we care about any funny animals on the internet. Cat memes are cute and all, but isn't emancipation truly hot? We often skip over this possibility when we contemplate creating kinship with animals, plants, or inanimate objects. Sometimes it's easier to sustain a conceptual relationship with a creature than it is to build a relationship based on respect with other humans, which is kinda fucked up. Still, we trust in the belief that any attempt to locate agency in nonhuman actors will help expand human consciousness or inspire such advances. As an architectural meme hive mind—a model of collective consciousness drawn from eusocial creatures, like bees or ants—building connectivity is the core of what we do. Memes are not an escape, but an amplification of what is here, now. We've found that dank memes really hit the cheetah spot, so we welcome all creatures in our blunt rotation. Go off, Kings!

—**Dank Lloyd Wright**, emerging theorist

WORLD OF TRANSFORMED AMBITION

"Shit," I winced as the ragged fingernail on my left pointer finger tore painfully back to the quick, caught on the stiff netting that protects the kale (the only green that grows without excessive effort). It's times like these I miss sidewalks and zippers—they made great emory boards. I gnaw away the remaining nail flap, enjoying the momentary patch of shade cast by an orbital behemoth drifting in front of the sun. I don't miss noise. I don't think anyone does. Later, while warm rain spatters thick leaves and soaks the naked ground, we'll spend hours laughing again at what once passed for ambition. It never gets old.

—**Trudy Watt**, architect and educator, Milwaukee

WORLD OF RELATIONABILITY

The Anthropocene bounds us to a history of capitalists, positivists, and settler colonialists who extract, spill, pillage, ravage, erode, capture, predate. In the Plantatiocene, Chthulucene, or Utopiacene, poetics of relation render us opaque. We are kin to the rebellious and the revolutionary. The exterminator builds architecture to wipe out our relationability: to the sky, to the earth, to the nonhuman, to the nonliving.

Against this utilitarian, functionalist, progressivist gospel, we dream of
radical ecologies of laziness,
listening to the song of birds,
to the sound of the future,
and the *cliquetis* of the wind through the cornfields.

—**WAI Think Tank**, educators and designers, planetary

WORLD OF CRTRS

new SNNN know very well:
BRRD heavens be WRRM hells

side SNKK wind from far road,
RB'BT hide dark down hole

one PR'SN too tall grow,
WNND and RNNN soon cease flow

fly N'SCT, but nest gone,
PLNT root seek water long

plenty LNDD left, shrink small,
FR'RR burn, destroy all;

old MNNN soul see and know:
as above, so below.

—**Andres L. Hernandez**, artist, designer, and educator, Chicago

WORLD OF DOORS

Door. Ajar and awake, deftly out of the way, so much hinges on this, our familiar exchange. Politely, it states, "after you, after you," and checks to make sure that we've all made it through. It returns to its jambs, where it patiently waits for its next chance to swing, to be flung, like a gate. When it speaks, it says things like, "come in," or "goodbye," or "please, I assure you, no need to be shy." It surprises me how much I simply adore, our give and our take, our lasting rapport.

—**Julia McMorrough**, architect and educator, Ann Arbor

WORLD OF ABOLITION

The world I want to live in is achieved through abolition and is one where maximal pleasure is available to all marginalized people and stripped away from those who currently have it. That world necessitates many more of us to engage in this abolitionism—of capitalism, of prisons, of homophobia, of white supremacy, of settler colonialism, of transphobia, of ableism, of animal consumption, of so much else I can only name in name, from my privileged perch. I want abolition and the forthcoming revolution to be simple as a choice to make individually and collectively. I want an intersectional current to make this wave swell toward socialism or anarchism and away from what is available to us, given to us by our white status quo plutocrats. I want to include all the marginalized and center them for the rest of my life, maybe for the rest of human existence, however long that is. I want you to see yourself in me and this work. Will you be my accomplice?

—**Andrew Santa Lucia**, designer and educator, Portland, OR

WORLD WITH(OUT) US

A world before us. A world after us. A world through us. A world beyond us. Forever in flux. Revolving. Evolving. Orbiting. Breathing. Living. Dying. Shapeshifting. A world beneath us. A world around us. A world within us. A world without us.

—**~~SANTIAGO~~ X**, artist, Chicago

12

Introduction: How to Be Friends with Architecture

The land grew and grew as she danced her thanks, from the dab of mud on Turtle's back until the whole earth was made. Not by Skywoman alone, but from the alchemy of all the animals' gifts coupled with her deep gratitude. Together they formed what we know today as Turtle Island, our home.

—Robin Wall Kimmerer

In what ways can an ethos of friendship catapult us beyond categories and distinctions, where notions of subjectivity and space are given permission to play themselves out in nonhuman-centric and nonnormative ways?

—Shun Yin Kiang

When you talk about making friends, you are usually talking about connecting with another human—but not always. Sometimes you are referring to a relationship with another animal, perhaps a dog, cat, guinea pig, or horse. Sometimes you may be lucky enough to make friends with a fictional character in a book or a film. You may have even crossed paths with someone who is friends with their car, or their musical instrument.

Making friends with various forms of nonhumans offers an opportunity to escape undesirable conditions of the existing human world and enter, even if temporarily, another world with different vantage points, sensations, and codes of conduct. J. R. Ackerley's 1956 memoir *My Dog Tulip* makes indirect reference to the difficulties of life as a single gay man in London after the Second World War, while focusing on his relationship to a female Alsatian companion, Tulip. In an analysis of the memoir, the literary scholar Shun Yin Kiang highlights Ackerley's observation of and curiosity about Tulip's urinating routines as a form of communication to illustrate the role that nonhuman companionship can play in breaking down human-centered perspectives on the world. Kiang writes, "To see Tulip's urine as something more than just urine, to fancy a world in which dogs sniff and men follow after them, is to re-imagine the world in which we live. Ackerley's investment in cross-species friendship, in other words, helps resist and revise conventional notions of self and space."[1]

While temporary inhabitation of a nonhuman, or more-than-human, world may be pleasurable in and of itself, it also provides an opportunity to practice or rehearse more desirable ways of relating to other humans. When you return to the human-foregrounded world, you might find your own human personhood in an altered state and relate to other humans according to shifted rules. The experience of expanding awareness to include another being's perspective may also expand your capacity for solidarity with other human beings.

In this book, we hope to expand your capacity for friendship and solidarity to include buildings as companionable creatures as we explore the ways that architectural design can enhance, and be enhanced by, such creaturely camaraderie.

When we speak of creatures, we cast an intentionally wide net. A quick internet search yields the following definitions: "1. An animal, as distinct from a human being"; "1.1. An animal or person"; "1.2. A fictional or imaginary being, typically a frightening one."[2] This net is already pretty wide: a creature can be human or nonhuman, real or imaginary. Yet a little extra scrolling expands the net even

---

1   Shun Yin Kiang, "Friendship; Or, Representing More-Than-Human Subjectivities and Space in J. R. Ackerley's *My Dog Tulip*," in *Creatural Fictions: Human-Animal Relationships in Twentieth- and Twenty-First-Century Literature*, ed. David Harman (London: Palgrave McMillan, 2016): 132.
2   Oxford University Press, Lexico.com, s.v. "creature," accessed March 21, 2021, https://www.lexico.com/en/definition/creature.

further. The etymology of the word reveals its root in the Latin *creaer*, meaning "to create," and its medieval meaning, circa 1300, is "'anything created,' hence 'a thing' in general, animate or not...from Old French *creature* 'created being; all creation' (Modern French *créature*), from Late Latin *creatura* 'a thing created; the creation; a creature,' from *creatus*, past participle of Latin 'to make, bring forth, produce, beget.'"[3] With this simple step backward in time we extract our justification for including architecture in the cauldron of creatureliness, into which all things animate and abiotic may be stirred.

In the Judeo-Christian context, the emphasis on creation refers to God's acts during a seven-day master class in manifesting the contents of "his" imagination—heaven, earth, and animals, including humans, who are conveniently set apart by their likeness to "him." This likeness was accompanied by humans' own preternatural skills of manifesting the tools and technologies that set us apart from the "nature" of Eden, and established an ecological hierarchy that kept us distinct and apart from the other creatures. Yet Indigenous creation myths such as Turtle Island offer alternative frameworks for conceiving of our relationships to nonhumans. As recounted by Robin Wall Kimmerer, when Skywoman falls from Skyworld into the dark water, the geese catch her fall, the turtle offers his back as her home, and the other animals gather mud to spread on his back to create the earth. Skywoman expresses her gratitude by planting fruits and seeds to feed them all.[4]

The reciprocity embedded in this myth of building home helps us to decontextualize the act of creation from the influence of the theological hierarchy established in the myth of Genesis, and replace it with a condition of relational co-creation, reintegrating humans (and architecture) back into the big melting pot of creaturely inclusion. We are indebted to the work of Donna Haraway, who has theorized, from the Western perspective, the ways that "significant other" forms of being as varied as cyborgs and companion species, such as dogs, challenge the definition of human that is derived from the Judeo-Christian creation myth in order to tell "a story of co-habitation, co-evolution, and embodied cross-species sociality."[5] While Haraway favors the word *critter* over *creature*, presumably to avoid association with the latter's creationist roots, we choose to stick with *creature* as a deliberate act of reappropriation, and to willfully acknowledge the active role that all creatures play in constructing each other's respective existence and reality.

The traditional anthropocentric approach of Western architecture tends to see architecture as an instrument of "civilized" culture. In this understanding, architecture is

3   Online Etymology Dictionary, s.v. "creature (n.)," accessed March 21, 2021, https://www.etymonline.com/word/creature.

4   Adapted from oral tradition, Robin Wall Kimmerer, *Braiding Sweetgrass: Indigenous Wisdom, Scientific Knowledge, and the Teaching of Plants* (Minneapolis: Milkweed Editions, 2013).

5   Donna Haraway, *The Companion Species Manifesto* (Chicago: Prickly Paradigm Press, 2003), 4.

a tool that addresses either environmental directives (provide shelter, deliver utilities, heat and cool occupants) or cultural ones (communicate an idea, support activities, establish collective lifestyle norms). Regardless of the problem, the logic it uses to rationalize a solution often follows a one-way arrow of cause and effect. Architecture is an object that does a thing in the service of its human occupants. We can't help but wonder, what if the arrow went both ways? What if our architecture was not a tool but a friend, a subject with its own experience of the world and its own set of needs?

We find an analogous reciprocity in the relationships between humans and horses. While the European paradigm casts horses as objects of value and power, civilizing tools of agriculture, transportation, and war, Indigenous cultures of North America revere horses as sacred companions who "help to heal the wounds that cause the mind, body, and soul to shift out of alignment," in the words of the scholar and journalist Yvette Running Horse Collin.[6] Running Horse Collin's work challenges the narrative, common in Western academia, that native horses died off in the Ice Age—a narrative that credits Spanish colonists with their reintroduction to the continent, erasing a deep, millennia-long interspecies connection and redefining horses as an implement of white culture. Her dissertation draws on fossil records and anthropological studies to show that the intimate relationship between Indigenous humans and horses has been maintained continuously for thousands of years.[7]

Brianna Noble, a horse trainer who rehabilitates rescued horses at her Bay Area ranch, describes the companionship that horses have to offer: "As fight or flight creatures, a horse's very survival relies on their ability to read the emotions and body language of its herd around itself. ...Mimicking our emotions, they put up a mirror that allows us to evaluate ourselves in an ever forgiving, nonjudgmental way." In this book, we attempt to replace the horse with architecture as the subject of this statement: What if architecture "put up a mirror that allows us to evaluate ourselves in an ever forgiving, nonjudgmental way," and what if we actually looked at what the mirror showed us and responded to it in a way that would help us address some of the crises facing humanity at this moment in time?

We ask this question with the ambition of building space for cultural imagination to envision a world on the other side of struggle, yet this process starts with the way our individual imaginations conceive of the relationships we enact on a daily basis. This is not a utopian ideal that we imagine, but rather an aspirational, intersectional response to the conditions that some refer to as the Anthropocene—the geological era that marks the start of irreversible human impact on the earth and its ecology, and whose root causes align with the same social, cultural, and

6   Shoshi Parks, "The Shared History of Wild Horses and Indigenous People," *YES!*, April 27, 2020, https://www.yesmagazine.org/environment/2020/04/27/native-horses-indigenous-history/.

7   Yvette Running Horse Collin, "The Relationship Between the Indigenous Peoples of the Americas and the Horse: Deconstructing A Eurocentric Myth" (PhD diss., University of Alaska, Fairbanks, 2017).

economic factors that have prompted many ongoing struggles for social justice. There is a balance to be struck between our efforts to halt the continued harm we are doing to our planet and our ability to adapt to the inevitable changes that our impact has already set into motion. Both will require a sustained, collaborative effort to reconceive and restructure the way that we think about our relationships to each other, to other species of animals, and to our environment.

We are architects, so architecture is the language that we speak; it is a language well-suited to worldmaking and storytelling, so we hope that these questions start to paint a picture of a different reality in which the causes of today's crises are less domineering, and to hypothesize a way that architecture may contribute to that future reality. We acknowledge that the practice of architecture can make significant, concrete contributions in areas such as resource consumption, land use, and housing, but we strongly believe that those efforts must be accompanied by radical cultural, social, and emotional transformations in how we all relate to the rest of the world.

We identify capacity to do this in a combination of conditions and ways of being that already exist in our shared reality and our imaginations, in culture at large, and in the culture of architecture. Collecting references and case studies from a range of sources, we use the following pages to position a possible way of seeing and being in the world that might actually already exist in the nooks and crannies of art, literature, internet memes, and our everyday lives. Something is stirring in our midst. We think that seeing both our human selves and our architectural environments as parts of an interconnected creaturely ecology may help us understand what that something might be.

The book is divided into three thematically distinct yet overlapping parts: Storytelling & Representation, Representation & Citizenship, and Citizenship & Symbiosis. Each of these parts consists of three components: an illustrated memoir recounted from architecture's vantage point, an essay, and a response. These three sets of chapters make a case for both *architectural creatures* and *creaturely architectures*. Parts 1 and 2 define architectural creatures as buildings or structures that look and operate like discrete actors and animate beings. Architectural creatures elevate the subjecthood and relationability of built matter alongside our own human personhood as peers, co-conspirators, and friends. Zoomorphism and animism help humans suspend the Western disbelief that abiotic entities (e.g., piles of bricks) can exhibit lively, sentient, and agential qualities—if a building looks like or behaves like an animal, it is easier to acknowledge it as companion. Parts 2 and 3 explore creaturely architecture as a broader quality of relationability that diffuses hierarchy and mixes up the identities of ourselves and our nonhuman companions. Creatureliness, as opposed to a discrete creature, no longer requires overt zoomorphism or animism to suggest its animate agency.

In Part 1, **Storytelling & Representation**, we look at the ways that architecture's formal language can mimic the shapes of things and beings in order to create narrative structures that inform our definitions of and relationships to self and others. In developing our case for architectural creatures, we explore the role of anthropomorphism, zoomorphism, and other morphisms in architectural history and contemporary architecture and speculate on the impact of formal resemblance in cultivating our capacity to relate to, interact with, and ultimately befriend architectural companions. Respondents Stewart Hicks & Allison Newmeyer take animate qualities of humans and animals (both formal and behavioral) and translate them into architectural and geometric strategies for space-making and interaction. Their contribution to this book reflects on the discipline's resistance to see faces or other animal likenesses in serious architecture, and they initiate conversations with a fiction writer and a facade consultant to liberate new associations among literary description and architecture's "facial" articulations.

In Part 2, **Representation & Citizenship**, we explore a range of architectural strategies beyond formalism that support our expanded definition of creatureliness. Contemporary interpretations of animism provide a way of seeing the world that justifies our inclusion of both human and architecture in the broad category of creature, and allows all types of creatures to reconstruct their identities within that radically inclusive umbrella of animate beings. Case studies of contemporary architecture practices illustrate the different roles that an animist architecture might play in redefining our sense of locomotion, belonging, and citizenship in the Anthropocene. Respondent Joyce Hwang expands the definition of nonhuman charisma to unpack its potential superpower for both fauna and architectural matter.

In Part 3, **Citizenship & Symbiosis**, we shift from the redefinition of individual identities and our expansion of belonging to explore the implications of those relational moves as we discover new collectives and forms of solidarity. With help from popular culture, we invent new languages of architectural love that promote our ability to live bonded, interdependent lives with other creatures with whom we share the world. Frederick Scharmen responds from the retrospective vantage of the year 2045, analyzing his archive of literary examples of human-architectural companionships in relation to the planetary strife and reconciliation of the decades to come.

The story of this co-creative symbiotic relationship can be told in many different ways, from many different starting points. We organized the parts of this book described above so that they may be read in a cohesive arc from cover to cover, but you may also choose to open to any of these parts and read it as a stand-alone piece. We offer you agency to choose your own reading adventure, and welcome you to organize an experience based on your interests and interpretations. ●

PART 1

STORYTELLING   &

REPRESENTATION

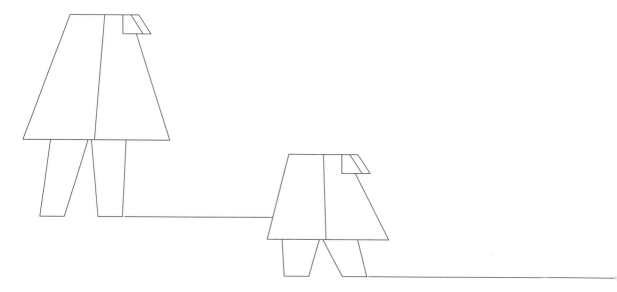

Of the Distant Past

From the Mouth of the Cave

There was a time long ago when we were all creatures. Regardless of our size, or what we were made out of, or how many legs we had, or whether we had legs or moved at all. You, the humans, were included in that mess, as were we, the dwellings.

All the creatures shared space on this rock, and we all had a place, more or less. The sharing was imperfect at times, but we had an arrangement to live within the fluid boundaries of the give-and-take. While not perfectly fair, or equal, or even pretty, an ebb and flow mimicked balance just enough to make the day-to-day uncertainties tolerable and keep the long-term uncertainties out of mind.

You humans were not the first creatures to alter that agreement. The dinosaurs also changed the game. But their dominance was more circumstantial than calculated, and their demise an unfortunate coincidence of the cosmos. For us dwellings, the real difference between you and the dinos was that many of them were too big to fit inside of us. Some were small enough to find shelter in our interiors, but the bigger ones would either leave us alone or play with us. They kept us on our toes, and they often kept us moving.

You were different because you wanted to tame us, to keep us still or at least restrict our movement, as you did with so many other cohabitating creatures when you wanted them to perform a task for you. You thought you were different because you walked on two legs (FYI, so does T. rex, as well as their descendant the chicken) and because you made tools (so do octopi and raccoons).

It was actually your fear that made you unique. All of us sharing this world felt a daily sense of unease that a bigger, stronger creature could come along and take our place. It was certainly not the case that you were the smallest or the weakest or the most in danger. But it was never enough that when threatened by someone with bigger teeth and claws, you could run on your two legs while throwing rocks and sticks with free hands, and then find one of us to hide inside of while the momentary danger passed. It wasn't a guarantee, but we did have a lot to offer you. Perhaps you found it unsettling when you came to us for safety and comfort and found another creature already cuddled up within our nooks and crannies. Maybe you were just jealous of our relationships with others, and wanted us all to yourselves?

I did feel special when you started paying extra attention to me. I liked it when you lit fires inside of me and warmed me up from the inside. It felt like the sun warming my exterior, except it was a warmth just for me. And when you drew on my walls, I thought I looked like you when you painted your faces. But my favorite thing was when you all gathered around the fire, pointed at the drawings, and gestured to the little ones as you told them stories about how we all came to be living on this rock together, and about all the wonderful, unpredictable things that could come to be when they would have their own children and grandchildren.

I suppose the unpredictability was unsettling for you. I liked it when an unexpected visitor came to share my shelter, or when a river changed direction and washed out my insides. I found it exciting when a friend from farther uphill suddenly came rolling down to fill up my openings with their little ones, and created new pathways to explore in my darker parts. I knew that these events upset you, but I could never have anticipated your response—the digging, the carving, the chopping away at all my parts, inside and out. You learned to make bigger tools, and your new drawings told different stories.

You domesticated the dwelling creatures by building your own versions of us. We had been your loyal friends for thousands of years, and you used our body parts to construct new dwellings who were at your beck and call, whom you could train to sit and stay at your command. You injected them with life that you could recognize and control.

But to us they have always appeared subservient, stagnant, and self-important; they seem to think they are better than us, more expressive, more complex, more predictable.

And yet they have moments when their playful, animated, fun-loving nature shine through, when they conjure memories of the days when their ancestors used to frolic with dinosaurs, cuddle with bears, or laugh at stories told by humans around the fire. These memories are most vivid during their interactions with the smaller humans, whose behavior has an uncanny resemblance to the old customs—playing with sticks, rocks, and other objects in ways that seemed to threaten the predictable stability revered by big humans, hiding in the nooks and crannies that otherwise collected dust, drawing on walls and telling them stories as if they could understand.

These moments shake the domesticated dwellings from their stupor of obedience, and against their better judgment provoke a response that surprises and delights the little ones. With a giggle, a shimmy, or a poke, they let their new friends know that they are alive and able to act of their own accord when the moment moves them, and that they appreciate the reminder of the fun that is available to them in the bigger, connected world. ●

Zoomorphism, or What Architectural Creatures Look Like

Power outage at Willis Tower leaves building looking 'disappointed,' just like everyone else in 2020

—*Chicago Sun Times* headline, May 20, 2020

Everyone realizing that the sears tower has a face is the only comedic thing that has happened this year

—Tweet by @topspittinwraps, May 20, 2020

The power went out @ Sears Tower and now it looks like some GD robot about to wreak havoc upon Chicago, and honestly, I wouldn't be surprised if that actually happened.

—Tweet by Karlee Kanz (@KarleeKanz), May 20, 2020

Figure 1.1. The Willis Tower exhibits a "face" following a power outage in May 2020. Photograph by Dan Fabry.

Sometimes it takes an extraordinary event to see something that has been staring you in the face your entire life. Like the fact that the Willis Tower (formerly the Sears Tower) has a face, and feelings to boot. This reality became apparent to residents of Chicago the night of May 19, 2020, when a storm flooded the tower's basement power station and caused an outage that darkened all but several emergency lights on its upper floors (Figure 1.1). It just so happens that these lights correspond with the tower's facial features, a pair of eyes and a mouth, which on this particular night clearly expressed the tower's annoyance at the downpour and resulting flood. The revelation of the tower's creaturely character provoked a reciprocal emotional response from fellow Chicagoans—and where some found humor and a pleasant sense of companionship, others recognized a fearsome menace hovering above the city streets. While it may have taken a dramatic unveiling to bring these psychodynamics to the forefront of their imaginations, it is likely that the city's residents have been harboring unconscious feelings about the tower for as long as they have walked in its shadow or climbed its heights.

Even in the absence of extreme weather intensified by climate change, it might be possible to notice a range of emotional responses that are prompted by the buildings you interact with on a regular basis: some instill a sense of comfort and well-being, some bring joy and amusement, and others are the source of aggravation and angst. These kinds of responses may be obvious or amplified in encounters with the extraordinary monumental architectures of cathedrals, civic institutions, or universities but also exist in our everyday environments, where they are likely more nuanced. The feelings evoked by our environments may be similar to the feelings evoked by our relationships with other beings—human or nonhuman, real or mythical, in our homes and surroundings or in our imaginations and stories. If we understand the structures and interiors of our built environment as having characters with personalities that we interact with consciously and unconsciously, then it follows that architectural design contributes to these relationships. By amplifying the idiosyncratic appearances and behaviors of our spaces through architectural forms that suggest creature-like appearances, we can highlight, edit, and redirect the stories of both our lives and our engagement with the world around us.

Zoomorphism is a representational or literary technique that attributes animal-like qualities, appearances, and behaviors to humans, objects, or other kinds of beings. Zoomorphic architecture has the power to increase our capacity to relate to and empathize with abiotic entities (like buildings), expanding our imagination so we can recognize them as creatures. In turn, it becomes a means to decenter ourselves in the narratives that shape our relationships to other cohabitants of the planet—human, nonhuman, and abiotic. As it stands, Western architecture is a largely anthropocentric discipline with a tendency to center a specific, white-male-European-human perspective in its design processes. The narrow bandwidth of this anthropocentrism has ramifications for the broader publics that use and engage architecture, including its role in perpetuating injustices related to social issues such as ableism, racism, classism, and environmental degradation. At this moment in our collective history, we are reckoning with these and other implications of the so-called Anthropocene for our lives and the lives of future generations. It is therefore of even greater consequence that we take seriously architectural forms of representation that support opportunities for redefining ourselves in relation to other creatures of this planet. Though it will not change discriminatory and exploitative policy, institutions or power structures, zoomorphism is one formal strategy that gives us an opportunity to practice seeing the architectures in our lives as companion creatures with whom we share the world, and by extension to challenge some assumptions about our role as humans on this planet.

At first glance, the Willis Tower may be an unlikely venue to discover zoomorphism in architecture. As a modernist building characterized by prismatic geometry, monolithic color and texture, and a lack of idiosyncratic articulation, the building resists any explicit resemblance with the animal kingdom.[1] The unexpected appearance of facial features on the tower's "head" reinforce the ease at which even the most non-creaturely-seeming buildings can come alive with animate personality. The Willis Tower's appearance and expression are neither purely human nor nonhuman. The blocky geometry of its overall profile is not congruent with the organic anatomy of any animal species and therefore pushes its visual resemblance into a more abstract and open-ended sense of animate ambiguity. This chapter will explore and unpack the many modes of zoomorphism for architecture, from on-the-nose reenactments (pun intended) to those whose suggestions are more ambiguous, such as the Willis Tower.

VULTURES, OR CARTOONISH MORPHISMS

> The expression "anthropomorphic" considerably underestimates our humanity. We should be talking about morphism. Morphism is the place where technomorphisms, zoomorphisms, phusimorphisms, ideomorphisms, theomorphisms, sociomorphisms, psychomorphisms, all come together. A weaver of morphisms—isn't that enough definition?
>
> —Bruno Latour[2]

The zoomorphic qualities of architectural creatures that exaggerate resemblances between animals and buildings are a means to an end, and not simply ends in themselves. The intent is not only to create explicit representations of animal form, but also to highlight and play with the fluidity inherent in the relationship between form and meaning. The application of zoomorphism in various art forms expresses this fluidity by articulating and amplifying the formal resemblances between humans, animals, objects, buildings, and landscapes, a wide set of techniques that Bruno Latour refers to as morphisms. Latour's observation is a useful reminder that

Figure 1.2. J. J. Grandville, *Mister Vulture*, from *The Public and Private Lives of Animals* (1867 edition).

---

1   While the Willis Tower does not typically suggest visual resemblances to animals, the tower's bundled tube structure is famously said to resemble cigarettes pushed out of pack at different heights.

2   Bruno Latour, *We Have Never Been Modern* (Cambridge: Harvard University Press, 1993): 137.

in the following pages when we refer to instances of either zoomorphism (beings or objects that take on animal-like qualities) or anthropomorphism (beings or objects that take on human qualities), the distinction is between techniques of representation that tell stories from different vantage points, and is not necessarily made by a hard line that defines what something is or is not.

Morphisms play a significant role in the narrative approaches of myth and literature. Anthropomorphism is a well-worn trope of children's literature where animals are portrayed wearing clothing, speaking, and engaging in typically human activities. Books for adult readers rarely depict nonhumans speaking with human voices,[3] but zoomorphic analogies that describe a character via a creaturely trait are common in various forms of writing (e.g., "she eats like a bird"). Yet zoomorphism can also be used to describe the actual physical form of a character in a story—the elephant-headed Ganesh in Hindu myths; in Greek mythology, Pasiphae's affair with a bull, which created the Minotaur; Gregor Samsa's overnight transformation into a giant beetle in Franz Kafka's *Metamorphosis*. In these instances of zoomorphism, the transition from human to animal form is critical to the development of a character and the narrative arc of the story. In other instances, it is not a human that takes animal form, but a physical location or landform. The monster Acheron, while referenced in various myths and legends in a range of forms and locations, has come to be associated with the underworld. In *The Book of Imaginary Beings*, Jorge Luis Borges relays a twelfth-century account of one man's direct encounter with Acheron as a zoomorphic manifestation of hell, a beast "larger than a mountain": "Its eyes shot forth flames and its mouth was so enormous that nine thousand men would fit inside. ...In this legend, Hell is an animal with other animals inside it." (Borges ends the passage on Acheron by quoting the eighteenth-century Swedish theologian Emanuel Swedenborg: "They tell me that just as Heaven has human form, so Hell has the form of a demon.")[4] There are also earthly examples of zoomorphism, such as Turtle Island, or the Kami,[5] a giant catfish who holds the islands of Japan on its back and whose movement is said to be responsible for seismic activity, or the Bahamut,[6] another fish at an even grander scale who is said to hold up a bull that holds a ruby that supports an angel who carries all of earth on its shoulders.

Within the visual arts, zoomorphism is often deployed as a tool of political satire. Certain approaches to caricature illustrate and exaggerate a human's character by depicting them with the physical traits of a specific animal. The graphic artist J. J. Grandville's oeuvre of proto-surrealist illustrations, for example, includes innovative, zoomorphic caricatures that comment on the absurdities of

3   Timothy Morton, *Humankind: Solidarity with Nonhuman People* (Brooklyn: Verso, 2017), 15.

4   Jorge Luis Borges, *The Book of Imaginary Beings* (1957; repr., New York: Penguin, 2005), 6.

5   Borges, 114.

6   Borges, 25.

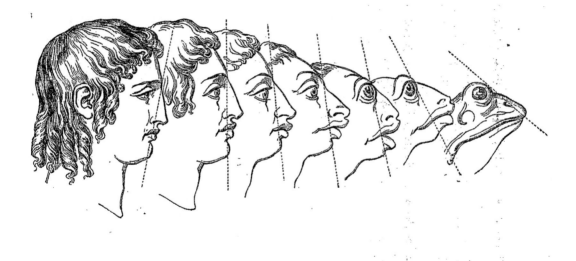

Figure 1.3. J. J. Grandville, *Portraits Compared*, from *Le Magasin pittoresque* (August 1844).

nineteenth-century French society.[7] Grandville's work is a useful point of reference to understand how zoomorphism, and other morphisms, conveys and challenges conventional and symbolic meaning in different contexts. In his best-known publication, *The Public and Private Lives of Animals*, Grandville presents the French bourgeoisie with animal heads directly substituted for human ones. For instance, *Mister Vulture*—who wears a top hat and fur collar and clutches a rent bill while hovering over a locked money chest—requires little explanation: the representation makes Grandville's opinion of landlords clear (Figure 1.2). In this example, zoomorphism has less to do with what any human actually looks like; rather, it communicates a quality of the character of landlords, connecting the landlord's role in society with conventional knowledge of how vultures behave.

Alternatively, in the drawing *Portraits Compared*, Grandville studies the relationships among the morphologies of different species by illustrating five transitional stages in which a human head might transform into a frog head: a human face with exaggerated lips and eyes that resemble a frog's becomes, in just a few steps, a frog face with a human nose and lips (Figure 1.3). In works that stray further from anatomical studies and push Grandville closer to the leaps of imagination and association central to surrealism, he includes inanimate objects in similar transition sequences. *A Promenade through the Sky* illustrates a parade of objects that follow each other through the clouds (Figure 1.4). The objects share enough visual likeness that the viewer accepts the sequence, but the leaps are actually quite surprising: from mushroom, to tree, to umbrella, to owl, to bellows, to spindle with thread, to the wheels of a cart pulled by three horses dashing across the stars. The progression is absurd and fantastical, and yet the logic is sufficiently established for

7   Patricia Mainardi, "Grandville, Visions, and Dreams," *Public Domain Review*, September 26, 2018, https://publicdomainreview.org/essay/grandville-visions-and-dreams.

Figure 1.4. J. J. Grandville, *A Promenade through the Sky*, from *Le Magasin pittoresque* (June 1847).

a viewer to play along with this game, which closely recalls the cloud watching we do when identifiable shapes come into and out of view as they drift across the sky.

Grandville's final publication, *Another World*, presents a collection of illustrations loosely held together by a minimal narrative structure: three main characters travel the universe collecting stories about the different worlds that they encounter, which are depicted in Grandville's drawings.[8] The collection builds on the morphological studies and strategies of Grandville's earlier work and continues his practice of commenting on the absurdity of everyday life, yet does so by recombining known objects and recognizable personalities into never-before-seen conditions and contexts. In these images, Grandville demonstrates the power of substitution, distortion, and association to build new worlds that are familiar yet simultaneously conjure unexpected possibilities and newness. In *A Conjugal Eclipse*, a collection of anthropomorphized telescopes gather to witness the personification of sun and moon in an embrace that creates an eclipse. In *A Bridge Leads From One World to the Next*, Grandville plays the role of cosmic civil engineer by imagining a physical connection between planets. Whether these games of morphisms are based on logics of meaning and association or purely visual likenesses, they stretch our imaginations beyond the boundaries of the categories and classifications that we use to make sense of the world (e.g., animal, vegetable, mineral), and remind us of both the arbitrariness of the boundaries and the exciting, playful, and potentially subversive connections that can be made when we break through them. And while Grandville plays these games in the realm of illustration, it is easy to imagine how these strategies could leap into the design of objects, buildings, and landforms.

These examples of morphisms in art and literature tell stories that comment on or challenge assumed definitions of human, nonhuman, vegetable, and mineral, along with the placement of humans in an ecological hierarchy, in search of alternative descriptions of reality. Instances of anthropomorphism or zoomorphism are not inherently good nor evil, but can be used to either reaffirm or subvert normative anthropocentric structures of knowledge and pursuits of desire, depending on their application.[9] Broadly speaking, a major theme in the history of Western architecture is the anthropocentric anthropomorphism that uses an idealized human form (that of the white European male) as the basis of architecture's organizational and formal logics. This creates a positive feedback loop between the assumptions that such architecture makes about human nature and aspects of the built environment that reaffirm those assumptions. But architectural zoomorphism has also made appearances throughout the discipline's history to challenge the feedback loop of anthropocentric anthropomorphism and offer alternative stories about our individual and collective desires and

8   Mainardi.
9   For more on the relationship between anthropocentrism and anthropomorphism see Wendy Lee-Lampshire, "Anthropomorphism Without Anthropocentrism: A Wittgensteinian Ecofeminist Alternative to Deep Ecology," *Ethics and the Environment*, Vol. 1, No. 2 (Fall 1996): 91–102.

ways of life. While anthropomorphism tends to privilege an idealized version of human nature (hence Heaven's representation as human form), zoomorphism exposes less virtuous dimensions of human and animal existence—aspects that are not necessarily evil or bad, but that speak to the typically unspoken shadowy, vulnerable underbelly of how we actually live in the world and who or what we dare to love. Of course, zoomorphism is also often associated with a sense of whimsy, humor, unseriousness, or childishness, and in that way can act as a Trojan horse to bring more unruly, unpredictable, or subversive content than might typically be permitted into the architectures that shape our lives in both public and private spaces.

RABBITS, OR ANIMAL ALTER EGOS

One way anthropomorphism and zoomorphism already enter our daily lives is through our morning bowl of breakfast cereal and the assortment of creaturely mascots who accompany it. These mascots might be thought of as mini Trojan horses (or even miniature architectures) that insert innocent-seeming stories (i.e., propaganda) into our morning rituals. And these stories bring with them assumptions about the meaning of anthropomorphic representation, assumptions that are open to reinterpretation and revision when we start to consider the fluid nature of morphisms.

If you were raised watching TV between 1959 and now, you probably know Tricks, the silly rabbit who has spent over sixty years trying to get his paws on a bowl of Trix cereal. When he does get a bowl, it is quickly taken away by children, who scold him: "Silly rabbit, Trix are for kids!" Unlike the mascots of other brands that sell sugary cereals to children, Tricks appears to be unable to enjoy the product that

Figure 1.5. Sethward, "Silly Kids, Trix are for Rabbits!," 2010. Courtesy of Sethward (sthwrd.com).

Figure 1.6. Trix cereal commercial, 1987. Use with permission of General Mills Marketing, Inc.

he is pitching. The simple pleasure that Tony the Tiger and Toucan Sam can take in freely eating their respective cereals raises the question of what makes Tricks different. It is natural to read all these characters as instances of anthropomorphism, the practice of endowing animals with the characteristics and behaviors of human beings—including the ability to talk, play sports, travel, and (except for Tricks) eat cereal. However, that Tricks is limited in this way suggests a different flavor of anthropomorphism, one marked by frustration and failure.

The nature of this difference is articulated and amplified in a 2010 comedy sketch posted on YouTube by actor and comedian Sethward, who appears as a disgruntled rabbit in a live-action version of the classic Trix commercial.[10] The rabbit Sethward portrays is sinister, obviously tired of getting pushed around by small children (actually adult actors) who deny him the cereal he wants. By the end of the video, the rabbit has knocked one kid unconscious and shot the other in the head; he finally has the last word, proclaiming, "Silly kids, Trix are for rabbits" (Figure 1.5). Sethward's exaggerated performance of the familiar narrative—Tricks wants and is denied Trix— contributes to a new reading of the original Trix cereal commercials as examples of zoomorphism, as opposed to the anthropomorphism that we would normally assume. This provocation prompts an important question: what if Tricks the rabbit is not an animal endowed with human characteristics, but rather a human *adult* taking on the form of a bunny? What might that say about a human adult's desire to consume a fruit-flavored, colorful cereal intended for children, and the lengths they will go to

---

10   Sethward, "Silly Kids, Trix Are for Rabbits!," April 1, 2010, YouTube video, 3:39, https://www.youtube. com/watch?v=VDrW7sc52Ck.

to get it? A 1987 Trix commercial begins with the rabbit in "Trix Land,"[11] a world populated by hundreds of other rabbits, all freely eating bowls of Trix cereal at all times of day (Figure 1.6). Tricks is euphoric and stunned when the other rabbits respond to a young boy in search of cereal, "Silly kid, Trix are for rabbits." Here we find the source material for the refrain Sethward's rabbit chants as he brutalizes the children. But in this version of reality, a world filled with other rabbits like him, the rabbit could have eaten his Trix in peace and avoided violence. Unsurprisingly, moments after Tricks is handed a bowl of his own, he is roused from sleep to find that "Trix Land" was only a figment of his unconscious, and once again he is denied the satisfaction of even a mouthful of cereal. Nevertheless, the fantastic reversal of reality depicted in Trix Land has a transformative potential that persists even as the truth is revealed. The dream has inserted a new narrative in the commercial audience's mind: another way is possible. And while the leap from a land of cereal-eating rabbits to creaturely architecture may seem large, we believe that zoomorphic architecture has the same potential to narrate another possible reality—one that moves away from scarcity and violence and toward fulfillment and pleasure.

HOMO SAPIENS, OR ANTHROPOCENTRIC ANTHROPOMORPHISM

Just as a zoomorphic cartoon can embody an adult desire to indulge in children's cereal, morphic architecture can also represent a collective desire for a future that is more joyful, playful, and connected to a broader world of creaturely relationships. A visit to Paleolithic France might help illustrate the role of architectural representation in evoking new future realities for our relationships to nonhuman cohabitants. In the cave paintings at Lascaux (ca. 17,000 BCE), Paleolithic hunters paid homage to the beasts they hunted with reverence and care and conjured the desired outcomes of their future confrontations. Interpretations of the paintings suggest that the hunters knew that invoking a successful hunt involved an equivalent acknowledgment of their potential for failure. As the architectural historian Spiro Kostof writes, the Shaft of the Dead Man appears to depict an unsuccessful result of one hunter's efforts: "The hunter, clearly, is the loser in the confrontation...[and the beast]...stands proud and triumphant over him even at the point of death."[12] In this scene, the hunter is portrayed as a zoomorphic stick figure with a bird's head or mask. Kostof reads the figure as an illustration of the Paleolithic worldview: humans were "insignificant in the face of universal and mystery-filled presence of nature...caught up in the flux and flow of life, moving with the herds...[with] a kind of timeless unfocused faith in the animal spirit."[13]

---

11   "Trix: Trix Land Commercial," June 19, 2015, video posted by user Mindless Shelf Indulgence, 0:29, https://www.youtube.com/watch?v=CMCF9bY2xAs.

12   Spiro Kostof, *A History of Architecture: Settings and Rituals* (New York: Oxford University Press, 1995), 25.

13   Kostof, 26.

The sense of reverence and connectedness of the Paleolithic human position vis-à-vis nonhumans suggested at Lascaux soon gave way to a new story: confidence in humanity's capacity to control and manage nature, as agriculture and animal husbandry facilitated settlement and the growth of cities during the Neolithic period. The philosopher Timothy Morton refers to this moment is history, as well as its continuing effects on our social and cultural lives, as "the Severing": a psychic and ontological break between reality as it is defined in human-centered terms and the *real*, the "ecological symbiosis of human and nonhuman parts of the biosphere."[14] For Morton, the rigid boundary of anthropocentrism that is introduced through agriculture and wrapped around our narrow definition of human existence interferes with our inherent solidarity with

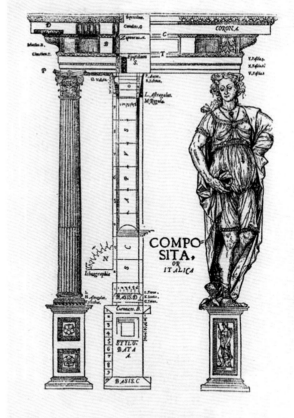

Figure 1.7. John Shute, *Composita*, 1563. Wikimedia Commons.

nonhuman beings.[15] From an architectural point of view, the Severing and its consequences are expressed in the anthropocentric anthropomorphism that is at the core of Western architecture. The architectural imagination of classical antiquity is often portrayed as a pinnacle of this outlook, with its compositional system of orders derived from the organizational logic of the human body. While none of the orders bares an explicit visual resemblance to the human form (with the exuberant exception of caryatids), each one is defined by a fixed overall proportion and ornamentation at base and capital often "seen as marking out the differences between people," as the architectural historian Carroll William Westfall explains, "from the rural rustic (Tuscan) to the sophisticated and highly decorated lady of the city (Composite) at the extremes and the heroic male (Doric), the chaste matron (Ionic), and the virginal young woman (Corinthian) in between."[16] The impulse to shape a building in relationship to human proportions and personality is derived from an assumption that human form is the ultimate expression of divine perfection in nature (Figure 1.7). This position was only strengthened through interpretations

14   Morton, *Humankind*, 13.
15   Morton, 15–16.
16   Carroll William Westfall, "Why the Orders Belong in Studio," *Journal of Architectural Education* 61, no. 4 (May 2008): 100.

of fifteenth-century Roman Catholicism and Renaissance humanism, which further elevated male human form as a representation of God's own image.

While the early modern movement promoted itself as a break from the traditions and symbols of classical architecture, a preoccupation with proportion and its relationship to the human body remained intact for many of its practitioners. Le Corbusier's Modulor (ca. 1945) updated Leonardo da Vinci's *Vitruvian Man* to create a system of architectural proportions that linked the scale of the male human body to geometric proportions found in nature. This touchstone of modernism reveals the continued imprint of classical anthropocentrism on architectural thought. More recently, scholars such as Charles Davis II and Irene Cheng have made important revisions to our understanding of modern architecture by exposing often invisible traces of racist anthropocentrism in its foundations. In his book *Building Character: The Racial Politics of Modern Architectural Style*, Davis connects the conceptualization of national architectural styles that were the precursors of modernism with contemporaneous scientific theories of bodily characteristics, race, and nationality. According to Davis, early modern architectural theorists used the taxonomic logic of the natural sciences to rationalize architectural styles as expressions of regional or national identities, replicating the racial hierarchies embedded in these theories. "Instead of interpreting the paradigm of architectural organicism as marking a precipitous break with the human-body metaphors of neoclassical theory," he writes, his work "examines the racialized human-body metaphors that were an implicit element of the scientific rationalization of architectural character."[17] Davis's analysis illustrates the continuity of architecture's Eurocentric anthropocentrism and its justification as a reflection of a natural order, despite its transition from a classical to a modern worldview.

Davis uses the term *character* interchangeably with *style* to describe an aesthetic architectural expression specific to national or racial identity and based on scientific taxonomies. However, *character* has been used differently in other contexts to push back against anthropomorphic standards of beauty and generate alternative forms of aesthetic expression. These other applications of architectural character represent one instance where a more explicitly subjective set of criteria has valued idiosyncrasy and composition above principles of geometric proportion tied to physiological studies.

COWS, OR BUILDING CHARACTERS

Historically, character in architecture is a quality that emerges from the relationship between a building's form (physical figure), its appearance and aura (sensual

---

17   Charles L. Davis II, *Building Character: The Racial Politics of Modern Architectural Style* (University of Pittsburgh Press, 2019), 15.

Figure 1.8. Jean-Jacques Lequeu, *Cow Barn and Gate to the Hunting Grounds*, 1815. Wikimedia Commons.

effect), and its meaning (the idea it conveys). In the eighteenth century, French neoclassical architects developed an approach that emphasized character by prioritizing the relationship between architectural form and its purpose. Character was "a means to shift the conversation from the structure itself onto the effects the structure has on its occupants and viewers," the architects Stewart Hicks and Allison Newmeyer explain. "This shift helped get the discipline out of a rhetorical jam brought on by the quest for perfection and ideal proportions."[18] Rather than applying proportions of the human body to architecture, "architects now tried to instill human characteristics into the buildings," the historian Emil Kaufmann writes of this moment, inaugurating "the era of *architecture parlante*—'Narrative' architecture."[19] Kauffman references the work of Claude-Nicolas Ledoux, and specifically his design for the royal saltworks at Chaux, as an example of *architecture parlante*. Ledoux used the unexpected composition of platonic solids, recognizable classical elements, and inventions of ornament to create buildings whose form would express the nature of their purpose. For example, the Oikema, or House of Love, provided sexual instruction within its phallus-shaped plan, and the inspector's house resembled a

18   Stewart Hicks and Allison Newmeyer, "Why We Got Into Character," *MAS Context* 32 (2020): 7.
19   Emil Kaufmann, "Three Revolutionary Architects, Boullée, Ledoux, and Lequeu," in *Transactions of the American Philosophical Society* vol. 42, part 3 (Philadelphia: The American Philosophical Society, 1952), 440–41.

Figure 1.9. Jean-Jacques Lequeu, *He Is Free*, 1798 or 1799. Wikimedia Commons.

giant eye, overlooking the river and grounds. The result was an architecture whose parts were able to "speak" on behalf of the whole. The significant contribution of *architecture parlante* was to decouple architectural form from both the direct imitation of nature and blind adherence to tradition. The redefinition of "natural" through the logics of purpose liberated architectural form to express the artifice of its composition via the manipulation and distortion of the classical status quo.

Another subject in Kaufmann's study, Jean-Jacques Lequeu, expanded *architecture parlante* by adding a new dimension to architectural character: the merging of architectural components with human and nonhuman flesh, such that architecture becomes an animate character itself. Lequeu's drawings use architectural rendering techniques to exaggerate the presence, vitality, and sensuality of life. In character studies of human facial expressions, enigmatic portraits of erotic bodies and genitalia, and fantastical architectural complexes, Lequeu's work equates organs, bodies, and buildings with commensurate spatial weight and narrative potential.

In a 1757 drawing titled *He Is Free*, Lequeu renders a nude woman on her back, limbs splayed, inching her way through the open lunette above a cornice supported by an array of stone heads with distressed expressions (Figure 1.9). She appears to be contorting her body to reach through the aperture to catch a bird, who is pecking at the architectural ornament; a pair of testicles trails from its tail feathers. The image raises more questions than it answers about the relationships between human, animal, and building. Is the building birthing this woman, whose sensuality is exaggerated by her gravity-defying breasts? Is the architecture-pondering bird a zoomorphic instantiation of Lequeu himself, fantasizing about how the female building desires his stone-crafting virility? While the exact plot remains enigmatic, this drawing is emblematic of Lequeu's broader contribution to architectural character: to challenge the strict binary distinction between soft biological bodies and hard, stone structures, and to dramatize how characteristics of desire (personal, sexual, or spatial) might prompt us to have more pleasurable relationships with our buildings.

What does it mean for architecture to *be* a character, rather than simply to *have* or *embody* character? In literature, characters are almost always animate beings, whether human or animal. This reinforces a conventional subject-object relationship in which living subjects affect inanimate objects. To be an architectural character, however, conflates a typical understanding of subjecthood and objecthood. While usually we conceive of buildings as objects (or piles or assemblages of matter) that implicate human subjects, if architecture is a character, then a building could be an active subject with a similar agency to that of humans.

Another work by Lequeu, a monumental cowshed in the shape of a cow that he captions, matter-of-factly, "the Cow Byre faces south on the cool meadow," introduces a type of architecture that is itself a character (Figure 1.8). Part sculpture, part building, this massive bovine replicates a cow's biology at a magnified scale and dresses it up with ornament and accoutrements, including three cowbells, an intricately patterned saddle, and a giant ceremonial urn atop its back. With its head tilted just slightly off axis, the cow surveys the landscape ahead, perhaps in the hopes of exchanging glances with livestock and cattle farmers seeking its shelter. Human and nonhuman animals that approach it can choose either to return its gaze in validation or reject its agrarian authority. While we assume that the Cow Byre houses bovine sleeping quarters, its interior is never revealed or described. The cowshed remains effectively an opaque monument in a field, companionable enough that we recognize its very familiar face and proffer a response, but aloof enough that we're not sure how to interact with it or inhabit its seemingly solid limbs and mysterious viscera.

The Cow Byre demonstrates how a building can be an animate architectural character in general, but it also points to a break in the Western canon, in which architectural character is tightly linked to anthropomorphism. Lequeu's rendering of his bovine friend is one of the first images in Western architectural history books that unabashedly embraces zoomorphism. Yes, residues of classical, anthropomorphic influences and the anthropocentric worldview that classicism represents persist here, but now an animal on all fours is the star of the show. Even the stumpy Doric column stubs that flank the cowshed's podium have been animalized and distorted for nonhuman consumption (literally), as if the cow took a healthy bite out of each one.

SPECTRUMS OF ZOOMORPHISM

(HIGH-FIDELITY / LOW-FIDELITY)

The Cow Byre defines one end of a spectrum of architectural zoomorphism. Buildings can look like and perform like animals in a broad variety of ways that differ in fidelity and form. High-fidelity zoomorphic architecture communicates an explicit reference to a known species, anatomy, or physiology. By translating the scale, material, or disposition of a recognizable animal into architectural terms (e.g., a superscaled bovine limb!), hi-fi zoomorphism invites the practice of new stories, relationships, and power dynamics among humans and our environs.

On the other hand, low-fidelity zoomorphic architecture conjures animate qualities but resists depicting or explicitly referencing a known animal. Lo-fi zoomorphism invites more open-ended and diverse interpretations by multiple audiences. Often, lo-fi zoomorphism prompts a "flickering"—the simultaneous or oscillating perception of multiple spatial conditions that destabilize a singular totality of legible architectural form.

Le Corbusier's iconic chapel Notre-Dame du Haut (1955), in Ronchamp, France, sits at the lo-fi end of architectural zoomorphism, opposite the hi-fi Cow Byre. While the Cow Byre's cow-like appearance is unmistakable, the striking form of the Ronchamp chapel makes an ambiguous gesture toward a creaturely profile while deliberately avoiding explicit reference to any one thing. According to the theorist Charles Jencks, Ronchamp "set[s] the mind off on a wild goose chase where it actually catches the goose, among other animals." Jencks also points out the chapel's resemblance to a boat, a set of praying hands, a nun's hat, and two figures embracing (Figure 1.10).[20] Le Corbusier explained that the sweeping roofline mimicked a crab shell that he picked up from a beach on Long Island.[21] These various interpretations (or explanations, in Le Corbusier's case) are subjective and prone to alteration with a change in viewing angle, or sunlight, or mood of the viewer. The nature of the building's formal composition lends itself to this fluid interpretation, an act akin to cloud watching. There is no single and perceptible defining gesture, but rather several gestures and the relationships between them that continually shift and morph as one moves around and into the building. The chapel is an aggregation of distinct parts that coalesce at moments to produce four radically different

---

20   Charles Jencks, *The Language of Post-Modern Architecture*, rev. ed. (New York: Rizzoli, 1977), 48–49.
21   Kostof, *History of Architecture*, 733.

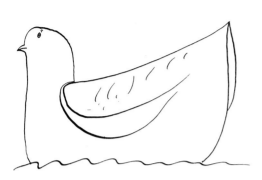

Figure 1.10. Hillel Schocken, "Methaphors of Ronchamp," 1972. Courtesy of Schocken Architects.

elevations, each of which reads as if it is a different building. The geometries of these parts vary from the irregular curvatures of the massive sweeping roofline to the straight, upright vertical towers topped with half-domed roofs.

BIOMORPHIC / GEOMORPHIC

The dialogue between organic and tectonic forms in the Cow Byre and Ronchamp place both projects in the middle of a second spectrum of zoomorphism that is defined by geomorphism on one end and biomorphism on the other. Geomorphic architecture tends to have geometric, mineral-like, or architectonic shapes. Geomorphic zoomorphism is often composed of profiles generated from simple geometric units or Platonic solids that have been added to, subtracted from, or reconfigured relative to one another. Zoomorphic architecture with a biomorphic bias tends to assume more anatomical shapes and often incorporates formal qualities akin to flesh, bones, or organs.

While Ronchamp is emblematic of the eccentric turn in the later part of Le Corbusier's career, his earlier work was committed to rationalism, and—along with his polemical writings—became a progenitor of the modern movement's quest for efficiency. Corb famously condemned the irrational, meandering paths of donkeys, thought to have produced the chaotic and congested plan of the medieval European city.[22] He argued instead for rational and orthogonal urban environments. At the architectural scale, with his "five points," Le Corbusier distilled the needs of the modern human subject into a formula that produces a healthful "machine for living." But these seemingly rational principles for mechanical efficiency may also be read as a formula for repressed, proto-creaturely desires. With pilotis as legs,

22   For more on the pack donkey's relevance to contemporary architecture, see Catherine Ingraham, *Architecture, Animal, Human: The Asymmetrical Condition* (New York: Routledge 2006).

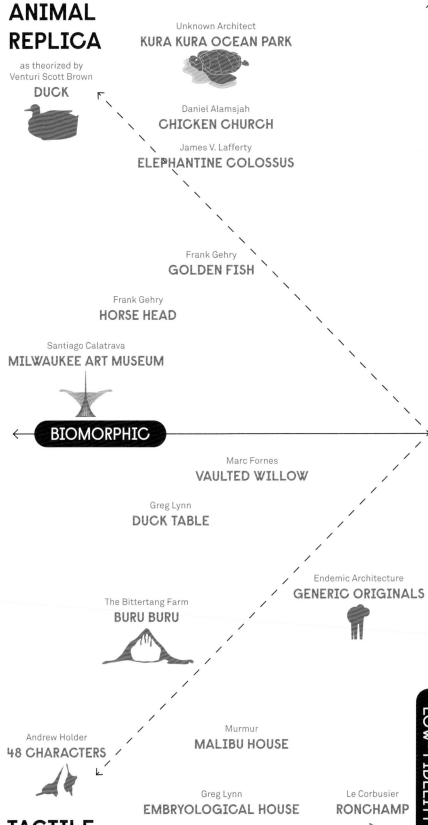

ANIMAL
REPLICA

Unknown Architect
KURA KURA OCEAN PARK

as theorized by
Venturi Scott Brown
DUCK

Daniel Alamsjah
CHICKEN CHURCH

James V. Lafferty
ELEPHANTINE COLOSSUS

Frank Gehry
GOLDEN FISH

Frank Gehry
HORSE HEAD

Santiago Calatrava
MILWAUKEE ART MUSEUM

BIOMORPHIC

Marc Fornes
VAULTED WILLOW

Greg Lynn
DUCK TABLE

Endemic Architecture
GENERIC ORIGINALS

The Bittertang Farm
BURU BURU

Andrew Holder
48 CHARACTERS

Murmur
MALIBU HOUSE

Greg Lynn
EMBRYOLOGICAL HOUSE

Le Corbusier
RONCHAMP

TACTILE
BODY

LOW-FIDELITY

**Figure 1.11.
Zoomorphism
Matrix.**

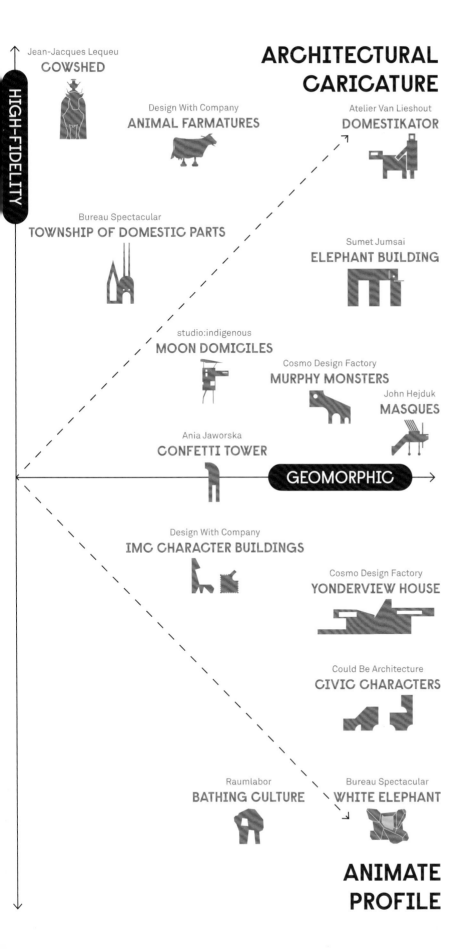

HIGH-FIDELITY

ARCHITECTURAL CARICATURE

Jean-Jacques Lequeu
COWSHED

Design With Company
ANIMAL FARMATURES

Atelier Van Lieshout
DOMESTIKATOR

Bureau Spectacular
TOWNSHIP OF DOMESTIC PARTS

Sumet Jumsai
ELEPHANT BUILDING

studio:indigenous
MOON DOMICILES

Cosmo Design Factory
MURPHY MONSTERS

John Hejduk
MASQUES

Ania Jaworska
CONFETTI TOWER

GEOMORPHIC

Design With Company
IMC CHARACTER BUILDINGS

Cosmo Design Factory
YONDERVIEW HOUSE

Could Be Architecture
CIVIC CHARACTERS

Raumlabor
BATHING CULTURE

Bureau Spectacular
WHITE ELEPHANT

ANIMATE PROFILE

WHAT ARCHITECTURAL CREATURES LOOK LIKE

Figure 1.12. John Hejduk, *Watercolor from Riga*, 1985. John Hejduk fonds, Canadian Centre for Architecture © CCA.

the ribbon window as a slit for eyes to look through, and the roof garden providing a spunky hairdo, the Villa Savoye might easily be seen as a stealthy crab-like creature, ready to shuffle away across the lawn at the first sign of trouble.

While it may be a stretch to classify the Villa Savoye as zoomorphic, it does help define the geomorphic end of this second spectrum of zoomorphism. The

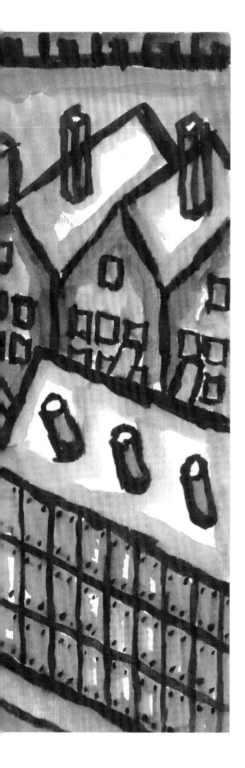

geomorphic language established by Le Corbusier's five points became the formal basis of John Hejduk's idiosyncratic *Masques*. These folly-sized architectural characters possess figural, zoomorphic profiles composed of architectural elements that negotiate between the anonymity of type and the eccentricity of personality. Columns become legs; spikes and antennae become hair; hallways and stairs become arms, noses, or other appendages. As deliberately vague abstractions, the Masques are loaded with affect, with ideas about narrative and character translated into creature-like form and activated in Hejduk's urban scenarios (Figure 1.12). A nomadic tribe of structures, each with its own distinct profile, character, and story, the Masques exist at a scale somewhere between a full-size building and a sculpture. Though born from the context of a specific place, they move freely, occupying and inventing new territories as they accompany Hejduk from city to city.

Another architect who tends to reproduce self-similar zoomorphic architectures in different urban contexts is Santiago Calatrava, whose work extracts functional and aesthetic lessons from the skeletons of animals to reproduce the effect of a lightweight frame with the capacity for locomotion. Calatrava's work helps define the opposite end of the morphism spectrum: the realm of biomorphism. While critics of Calatrava's work focus on its budget-busting extravagance, supporters argue that it is not simply biomorphic (having the appearance of biological forms), but also biomimetic, with a formal logic linked to material efficiency derived from its application of principles found in nature. Calatrava's World Trade Center PATH Station (2016), in New York City, uses an array of exposed structural fins to create a form that perches on the crust of the earth like a dinosaur reconstructed from fossils, with spiny appendages growing from its back that suggest either armored plates or wings. One feels as if a specimen from the American Museum of Natural History has walked five miles south from its home next to Central Park to hang out downtown. This project (and many others by Calatrava) constrasts its urban context by standing in for a version of "nature" that is in opposition to the artificial, gridded geometries of human-made constructions in the city. Supporters of Calatrava's buildings sell their resemblance to organic phenomenon and their self-serious study of physical laws of nature as evidence of structural and material efficiency.[23] But while their forms are sculptural and expressive, they are based on the carcasses of dead animals; they lack not only skin, feathers, and facial features, but also character and personality.

In Figure 1.11, these two spectrums of zoomorphism define two axes of a matrix that describes a field of possibilities for what zoomorphic architecture can look like and narrate. Each of the four quadrants is named for its defining characteristics and effects and contains examples of projects that illustrate those qualities.

ANIMAL REPLICAS

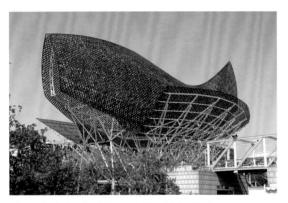

Figure 1.13. Frank Gehry, *Golden Fish*, 1992. Wikimedia Comons.

High-fidelity, biomorphic architecture is what we call "animal replicas" (positioned in the upper-left quadrant of the matrix). These projects tend to be sculptural, three-dimensional reenactments of familiar animal bodies, like the Long Island Duck made famous by Robert Venturi and Denise Scott Brown.[24] An animal replica often leverages its explicit shape to communicate something important about the building's function or identity; for example, the Long Island Duck is a roadside outpost where a duck farmer sells duck meat and eggs. By taking on an animal's explicit shape and likeness (e.g., a duck), albeit at a much larger scale and in different materials (here, stucco instead of feathers), animal replicas communicate purpose without the need for any sign, logo, or text-based explanation. Most examples of animal replicas fall outside of the traditional canon of architecture, and instead could be classified as pop-novelty buildings, spectacles, or landmarks that attract an existing audience, like the Fresh Water Fishing Hall of Fame in Hayward, Wisconsin,

---

23 Contrary to this argument, Calatrava's work has been criticized (and fined) on numerous occasions for issues related to scheduling delays, cost overruns, failures to meet health and safety codes, and structural deficiencies. In 2019, he was fined $87,000 by an Italian court for his design of Constitution Bridge in Venice, Italy for "cost overruns and 'negligence' in faulty design," due to weakness in the steel and glass structure. See Sydney Franklin, "Venice fines Santiago Calatrava for slipper, inaccessible bridge," *Architect's Newspaper*, August 12, 2019, https://www.archpaper.com/2019/08/venice-slippery-bridge-fines-santiago-calatrava/.

24 Robert Venturi, Denise Scott Brown, and Steven Izenour, *Learning From Las Vegas*, rev. ed. (Cambridge, MA: MIT Press, 1977), 17.

Figure 1.14. Unknown architect, Kura Kura Ocean Park, 2008. Photo by @jaladrone and @harieskndr.

or the giant turtle of Kura-Kura Ocean Park, a beachside aquarium in Central Java, Indonesia (Figure 1.14).

Animal replicas recall caricature illustrations like J. J. Grandville's *Mister Vulture*. Just as the bird of prey's easily recognizable head directly replaces the human head to convey Grandville's opinion of landlords, animal replicas in architecture replace conventional building anatomy with sculptural and scenographic animal anatomy in order to communicate an important character association or to offer cultural commentary about a building's identity.

Since the early 1980s, when he began making lamps that look like fish, Frank Gehry has used the form as inspiration for a range of objects, sculptures, pavilions and buildings. Gehry attributes his obsession with fish to early childhood memories of his grandmother storing the live carp she bought from the market to make gefilte fish in her bathtub.[25] The fish became his muse, a guiding force in the development of his architectural language. His most famous fish project is a pavilion built in Barcelona for the 1992 summer Olympics (Figure 1.13). Though lacking any specific features, the fish form is clearly articulated, and therefore the project sits in the animal replica quadrant, just above the horizontal dividing line between hi-fi and lo-fi. Although it is certainly possible to read the fish reference as some kind of joke, it is likely more accurate to describe it as a caricature of architecture (as

25 Kelsey Campbell-Dollaghan, "Frank Gehry at 83: Still Obsessed with Fish," *Fast Company*, January 14, 2013, https://www.fastcompany.com/1671622/frank-gehry-at-83-still-obsessed-with-fish.

opposed to an architectural caricature, discussed below). As in much of his work, Gehry devotes his attention to expressing the structure and skin of this pavilion. He is very explicit that the fish is architecture (like Grandville's vulture is human)—it has all the parts that one would expect architecture to have, including stairs and a circulation path. And yet its whimsical form contradicts our expectations of what architecture looks like. "Fish-like is what architecture could have been, had it taken a different direction than the anthropomorphic one, represented by the legacy of classical architecture," the theorist Emmanuel Petit suggests, reading into Gehry's intention. "Gehry turned his attention to a time prior to the classical architectural tradition; the fish might appear funny to us, precisely because we have been conditioned in that tradition."[26] Gehry's own words on Palladio help to clarify: "Palladio faced a fork in the road, and he took the wrong turn. ...He should have recognized that there's chaos. ...He would have been a pioneer."[27] The preclassical sensibility that Petit and Gehry both refer to is free of anthropocentric hierarchies, a chaos in which humans were one among many creatures, and therefore the structures that they inhabit (and their representations of the divine) were not bound to represent the human form but could expand to other creaturely beings.

(TACTILE BODIES)

Low-fidelity, biomorphic architecture is what we call "tactile bodies" (positioned in the lower-left quadrant). These projects delight in the fleshy, fatty, and supple imagery of living body tissue and organisms. As physically materialized architecture, they don't necessarily reenact the material qualities of flesh, but rather transmute its affect. Sometimes cuddly and sometimes grotesque, tactile bodies resist mathematical, geometric description and instead embrace the language of character traits and creaturely relationships.

Tactile bodies invoke the techniques of Grandville's series of morphological studies, which present iterative transitions between species and things. Just as Grandville's illustrations—for example, *Portraits Compared* or *Man Descending towards the Brute*—draw attention to the anatomic affinities and arbitrary distinctions between categories of beings, tactile bodies in architecture celebrate the ambiguity and fluidity of identity among morphologies of space.

For example, Andrew Holder's *48 Characters* is a collection of plump and fleshy sculptural objects created via plaster cast inside latex balloons and then manipulated with hand tools (Figure 1.15). No set of discrete geometrical or disciplinary

---

26   Emmanuel J. Petit, "The Other Architectural Manifesto: Caricature" (conference paper presented at Bauhaus University, Weimar, Germany, April 24–27, 2003), 9, https://doi.org/10.25643/bauhaus-universitaet.1283.

27   Quoted in Petit. The quote comes from a conversation relayed by Kurt Forster; Forster and Francesco Dal Co, *Frank O. Gehry: The Complete Works* (New York: Monacelli Press, 1998), 10.

parameters can fully describe his bulbous objects, but, as Holder writes, "what formal analysis struggles to rationalize, the languages of character and posture easily accommodate."[28] He intentionally designs his "characters" to prompt awareness and understanding of their bodily positions and personalities. Holder contends that his work is "an assault on the humanist position," arguing that the fictional animalistic vitality and otherworldliness of his characters deny an anthropocentric subject-object relationship such that "the human position is crowded out by this other position."[29] If character's architectural roots stem from a physiognomy of form as manifest in the classical orders, Holder's characters instead suggest a non-facial physiognomy composed of what Amy Kulper, writing in *Log* 31, calls "not-fingers and not-noses...lumps, protuberances, digits, and bulges." While ambiguous in their "species specificity," the characters of *48 Characters* definitively suckle, sprawl, squeeze, and snuggle.[30]

Tactile bodies like *48 Characters* define a pole of architectural zoomorphism characterized by smooth, organic wholes, where individual body parts are absorbed

28   Andrew Holder, "The Stories Bricks Tell Themselves," *Pidgin* 16 (November 2013): 8.
29   "Possible Mediums Panel: Tactile Objects," February 28, 2013, video posted by knowltonosu, 1:17:46, https://www.youtube.com/watch?v=PPe2v67FfeQ.
30   Amy Kulper, "Out of Character," *Log* 31 (Spring/Summer 2014): 90–91.

Figure 1.15. Andrew Holder, *48 Characters*, 2013.

into totalizing curves. This species of architecture is a descendent of Greg Lynn's work in "blob architecture," which embraces the physics of air, motion, and forces among gravitational bodies to establish vectors that define the logic of parts to whole in fluid, transitional ways, eliminating hard joints or corners that are typical in more conventional architectural tectonics. More than twenty years after Lynn's early experiments in this mode, the aesthetic qualities of blobs are "normalized" such that the computational process of their creation is no longer in focus; rather, the effects and affect-producing possibilities of these smooth, organic techniques are being pushed. Where blobs were once "embryological," always emerging and yet to be fully defined as definite beings, tactile bodies provocatively capitalize on their still-vague zoomorphism to create a novel yet approachable formal language that might entice new audiences to engage with innovative architecture.

ANIMATE PROFILES

Low-fidelity, geomorphic architecture is what we call "animate profiles" (positioned in the lower-right quadrant). These projects position figural silhouettes of architectural parts that enact character and imply locomotion and vitality. In comparison to their higher-fidelity "caricature" counterparts (see below), animate profiles are less explicit in referencing singular animal images or behaviors. They leverage simple geometric parts to initiate visual games that compel onlookers to interpret, narrate, and otherwise participate in making figural and mythic sense out of what they are seeing.

Bureau Spectacular's *White Elephant* is a flippable, tiltable small architecture that tumbles to accommodate various needs and desires (Figure 1.17). Without a fixed footing in the ground or floor, it is liberated from typical constraints of plan or section. The elephant can assume multiple figural stances—it is a single entity animated by eight different animate profiles. Human viewers may ascribe a distinct personality, temperament, or emotion to each postural orientation. Sometimes it menaces. Other times it seduces. Still other times, it jokes. Its multifaceted figural qualities demand spectatorship and make the viewer consider it from all angles and orientations. By defining the low-fidelity pole of geo-zoomorphism, *White Elephant*'s animality remains ambiguous and therefore in the purview of its inhabitants to define. Its polygonal, faceted geometry is far removed from the organic curves that articulate animal anatomy. Instead, its kinship with animals comes through its name and narrative. It prompts its inhabitants to empathize with its abstract postures and interpret the personalities of its perches through simile as opposed to resemblance; for example, it looms upright like a standing bear, or it crouches coyly like a cat (Figure 1.16). It offers a capacity for zoomorphic relationships and analogies as opposed to visual verisimilitude (its cowhide pattern notwithstanding).

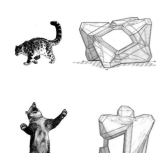

Animate profiles are influenced by R. E. Somol's writings on what he calls "saturated shapes" and the potential for architecture with graphic qualities to coalesce new audiences around "logos." In shape or logo projects, the whole is privileged above its parts, and despite its easy, legible profile, this whole does not offer any explicit reading or meaning. Logos are performative rather than descriptive: "They don't represent anything...but they might, under certain circumstances, *do* something."[31]

Figures 1.16 and 1.17 (below). Bureau Spectacular, *White Elephant*, 2011.

While animate profiles share certain qualities with an architecture of shape, several characteristics render them distinct, with their own identity: a legibility of parts that produces tension within the clearly outlined profile of the whole; an interest in the multiplicity of subjective experiences or interpretations of the profiles' disposition or character; a suggestion of narrative that situates an individual character within a larger collective context; the application of graphics or colors in opposition to constituent parts that creates another layer of disruption in the reading of the whole; a tendency among animate profiles to gather in groups. The overall effect of the animate profile is defined by intensity, intimacy, immediacy, and interaction. Animate profiles are inner-worldly and gregarious—emerging from the depths of dreams and fantasies, they are monsters in closets from our favorite horror stories, as well as imaginary friends.

Animate profiles learn from and enact the effects practiced by Grandville in his series of illustrations in the spirit of his *A Promenade through the Sky*, where a circuitous sequence of beings and things stage a game of visual association based on dreamlike, interpretative relationships. By soliciting multiple legible figures within a single silhouette, animate profiles in architecture invite people to move

31   R. E. Somol, "Green Dots 101," *Hunch* 11 (Winter 2006–07): 37.

Figure 1.18. Atelier Van Lieshout, *Domestikator*, 2015. Courtesy of Atelier Van Lieshout.

around them in space as different images snap into and out of optical alignment. It's an architectural game that everyone can play, with ample opportunity for return visits that apply new references.

(ARCHITECTURAL CARICATURES)

High-fidelity, geomorphic architecture, on the other hand, is what we call "architectural caricatures" (positioned in the upper-right quadrant). These projects tend to be more abstract than animal replicas because they translate or distort the organic qualities of bodies from the animal kingdom into more angular, Platonic, or regularized geometry native to conventional architectural drafting.

Nevertheless, architectural caricatures still use their shape and composition to communicate an explicit similarity to animal form or behavior. For example, Joep Van Lieshout's *Domestikator* is an inhabitable, architectural sculpture composed of boxy forms that clearly depict (and maybe even poke fun at) two bodies having sexual intercourse (Figure 1.18). While the exact human or nonhuman animal identities of the sexual partners are left open to interpretation, the intimate, animal act that they are engaged in is visually and compositionally explicit (so explicit, in fact, that the sculpture was banned from an outdoor exhibition at the Louvre, only to be picked up by the less prudish Centre Pompidou). Architectural caricatures position exaggerated yet explicit zoomorphism to make people laugh or cringe, often at the same time.

Like Grandville's *Another World*, where a cornucopia of abiotic beings are animated in intense encounters with one another that make palpable a range of sociopolitical projections (e.g., a personified Sugar Cane beating the blood out of an unfortunate Sugar Beet in a race for dominance of the sweetener market), architectural caricatures converge insightful observations about the world as it exists with seriously funny conjectures about other worlds of our desires.

For instance, Design With Company's *Animal Farmatures* lets animatronic creatures loose into the agrarian landscape of the American Corn Belt (Figure 1.19). These livestock-shaped, overscaled farm implements simultaneously cultivate farmland and entertain adjacent interstate car travelers and future high-speed cross-country rail passengers. Each of the farmatures is stuffed with technological apparatuses, six beast-machine mash-ups that cleverly couple animal anatomy with mechanical functions. For example, the Cow Combine's head serves as the "primary intake unit"; its "teeth" cut grain from the stalks and ingest it for further processing.[32] Threshing and winnowing occur within an abdominal cavity, and for full comic effect, the fully "digested" grain berries are expelled by conveyor belt through an aptly located anal aperture.

Drawing explicit cues from Lequeu's Cow Byre, *Animal Farmatures* re-stakes a claim in the theory of *architecture parlante*—buildings that use symbolism and pictorial reference to explain their function and identity. Architecture parlante is perhaps the ultimate manifestation of caricature in architecture: it exploits perspicuous visual likeness to communicate ("this building is for cows!"), it exaggerates the scale of familiar elements to produce laughter and surprise ("that cow is much too big for this pasture!"), and it indulges in bodily forms to insinuate sexuality and to project personality ("is that cow attracted to me?").

---

32 Stewart Hicks and Allison Newmeyer, "Animal Farmatures," *Life at the Speed of Rail Competition* (New York: Van Alen Institute, 2011).

CREATURES: ZOOMORPHIC CHARACTERS

Not all zoomorphic architecture is creaturely, and not all architectural characters are creaturely. Architectural creatures evoke a capacity for coming to life through a confluence of zoomorphic formal embellishments and fictional enhancements. Creatures exhibit physical and behavioral characteristics that are familiar, qualities like personality, posture, facial expressions, style, taste, charisma, and attitude; yet they occupy the world in unusual and surprising ways, enacting lively relationships between what something looks like and how it operates. Creatures are hard to pin down; they are representations, often ambiguous, of animate beings—not necessarily mobile, but projecting a presence that suggests they could get up and walk away at any time.

Grandville's caricatures and zoomorphisms rehearse lively relationships and interactions among beings that are not permitted by the rules of our existing anthropocentric world. As the title of his final book suggests, another vibrant world (or worlds) abounding with lively biotic and abiotic beings coexists with our own, if only we unlearn and dismantle the anthropocentric blinders that prevent us from seeing, experiencing, and enjoying them. Architects have long been aware that they participate in the building of the world, but Western architectural practice and thinking stop short of engaging relationships with the *worlds of their buildings*. Buildings live and act in their own worlds that overlap with and perforate our own, as was revealed to Chicago residents the night the Willis tower lost power. Because these "buildingly" worlds don't look human (or animal) and are not readily accessed by "grown-up" human storytelling modes, they too often remain unrecognized and autonomous to themselves. By rendering their sentient, animate, and lively qualities more explicit, zoomorphism (and other morphism) offer a narrative entry point for architects, and a broad public of everyday building users, to acknowledge and access the companion worlds of their buildings. ●

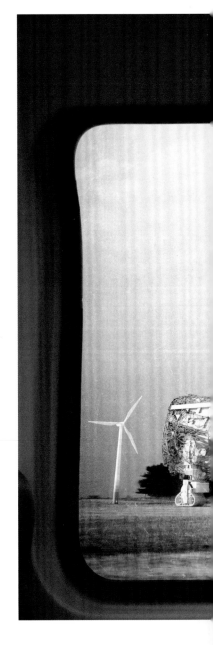

Figure 1.19. Design With Company, *Animal Farmatures*, 2011.

ALL EYES ON ARCHITECTURE

Stewart Hicks & Allison Newmeyer

We[1] wish architecture had something like a Rorschach test. You know, the test where inkblots on cards are used to gauge one's mental and emotional state. They are particularly useful in cases where a patient's emotional functioning is difficult to assess because of their reluctance to describe their thinking processes clearly and openly. People's reactions to being shown the vaguely animalistic shapes of the inkblots can reveal a lot. Even a refusal to play along can be useful to the psychologist's analysis.

This is the state we[2] find architecture in today—trapped in a pathological and persistent refusal to acknowledge or recognize the zoomorphic qualities of buildings, even by the very architects who designed them. To be honest, at first, we[3] thought it was a problem on our end. Maybe the animals and faces we were seeing everywhere were due to an underlying psychological disorder of our own. To confess, given some of our early childhood experiences, this is a real possibility. I[4] used to meet my friends at a location we called "the nose of the earth," a name that reflected an unrealistically scaled reading of a small dirt mound. And me,[5] well, I thought Henry David Thoreau's description of Walden Pond as the "earth's eye" was a literal description of its shape, including the surrounding trees, arranged like eyelashes.

---

1   Stewart Hicks and Allison Newmeyer.
2   The collective "we" of architecture.
3   Stewart Hicks and Allison Newmeyer.
4   Allison Newmeyer.
5   Stewart Hicks.

But over time, we've[6] collected enough evidence to prove it isn't us; it's architecture. This chapter is a collection of some of this evidence: experiences, friendly conversation, and works of others, together in one place to showcase the underlying pathology and complemented by some examples of healthy reactions and attitudes. Much of this collection is written in the first person, so we've used footnotes to declare the changing nature of the "I"s. Some of the "I"s are architects, but some are people outside the field; their inclusion is an attempt to model the kind of healthy behavior we would like to see in architecture. The collection does not include the obvious advanced architectural body metaphors: caryatids, circulation, "sick" buildings, structure and bones, cladding, and so on. Rather, we stick with a loose associate of buildings and eyes for, you know, transparency.

This collection took some time to compile. At the outset of our architectural adventure, we[7] reluctantly played along with the typical brainwashing and deprogramming techniques of architecture school, like when they make you draw orthographic depictions of potatoes. This task is impossible to approach head-on. The only solution is to invent a translation strategy that relies less on "representing" what is apparent visually and more on conveying deep structural concepts embedded in the object, which become filtered through the mechanics of drafting. For instance,

the potato's shape, eyes, and lumpy features lack distinct definition and are impossible to measure directly with a ruler. Fittingly, these qualities also make the potato particularly enticing to anthropomorphize—George Lerner's translation to Mr. Potato Head is a natural step.

To map these immeasurable and ill-defined features onto a flat sheet of Arches brand watercolor paper using HB lead and a parallel rule is a challenge. My[8] compromise was to graphically slice up the potato and splay it open flat, so it would look like a flower, with each eye meticulously mapped to its corresponding petal. When informed that this particular choice strayed too far from the reality of the potato, I pleaded the tuber's desire to masquerade as a flower once in a while.

I[9] remember there was always talk about this potato assignment—it was a legend of sorts. The mysteriousness was amplified because Stewart wouldn't show me the drawing, even though I asked. He was probably self-conscious because the word on the street was that it looked like a marijuana leaf. A few years later, the same "potato teacher" was on my design review. The project was housing composed of only internal windows. It was a series of openings; the occupant would travel through the unit and pick their own aperture adventure. By the time I got to the design of the exterior, I

---

6   Stewart Hicks and Allison Newmeyer have.
7   Stewart Hicks and Allison Newmeyer.
8   Stewart Hicks's.
9   Allison Newmeyer.

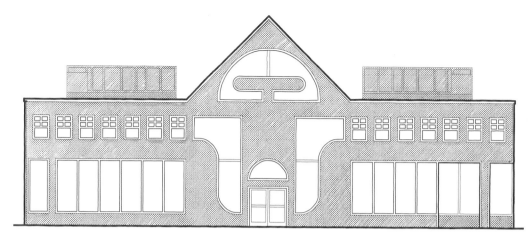

Figure 1.20: Stanley Tigerman, Anti-Cruelty Society Building. Illustration by Design With Company.

was out of window ideas. At the pin-up, the potato teacher ended the review with the question, "Are you serious about that elevation?" It was a blank wall with two smaller windows above a single larger one. To me, it was perfectly logical—two for bedrooms, a bigger one for living. There was no explanation or conversation with the other jurors, only a strong implication I shouldn't be serious.

During lectures in history class, I[10] would flip to the last page of the textbook to look ahead to find what the point of all this was, like someone eager to ruin the ending of a novel. There was a grainy black-and-white image of Stanley Tigerman's Anti-Cruelty Society Building, in Chicago, in the top-left corner (Figure 1.20). I must have read that single page a dozen times. In my mind, somehow all of architectural history culminated right there, and it represented the potential escape from the potato's gravitational pull, toward a healthier attitude.

Stanley writes,

> The Society wished to change that image (euthanizing attitudes), replacing it with one concerned with adoption. Thus, semiotically speaking, the new building is a sign, a billboard, that is intended to advertise the new message. The principal elevation recalls the traditional form of apartments over a store. Above storefront windows (the old "doggie in the window'" trick), the fenestration is comprised of a double-hung sash. The exterior is clad in horizontal aluminum siding, prefinished grey with white trill. The entrance is marked by a Palladian cutout, a key to a can of dog food and windows like the cheeks of a basset hound.[11]

After graduation, I[12] worked a block away from the Anti-Cruelty Society. It sits on LaSalle Street, and I was on Dearborn. During lunch hours, I visited

---

10   Stewart Hicks.
11   Stanley Tigerman, "The Anti-Cruelty Society," *Oz* Vol. 4 (1982). https://doi.org/10.4148/2378-5853.1041
12   Stewart Hicks.

to study the composition of the facade and to pet the animals. I ended up adopting a cat, Lola, from the shelter, as a birthday present to Allison. Lola passed around the same time as Stanley, in 2019. They were kind of related—with both of them, affection was pretty hard to come by. When we[13] arrived in Chicago the second time, we visited Stanley's office looking for advice and his blessing, and we left after he told us to get an architectural license and that we moved around too much (he was skeptical of our commitment to the city). The relationship with Stanley began sprouting only after we shared a seat on a panel discussion with him, backdropped by a gallery lined with dozens of scans from sketchbooks he kept over the years.

These repressive attitudes and pathologies are not limited to school assignments, nor to the short period of time we were students. During a recent conversation between Michael Meredith,

of MOS Architects, and John McMorrough, of studioAPT, posted on the Instagram feed "Practice Architecture Talks" (@practice_architecture_talks), McMorrough hesitantly brought up how MOS's Brick House kind of looks like a crooked devil face with horns (Figure 1.21). The subject was broached only after the cushioning pre-apologies one would expect when segueing from a close and lengthy examination of the challenges in choosing a structural system. That McMorrough was reluctant to have the conversation venture into such matters underscores how deep, yet murky and awkward, this line of conversation can be for architects.

Eager to build a robust foundation of lesser known yet acceptable precedents and buffer himself with a protective wall of related historical anecdotes, Meredith sourced a possible osmotic transfer to his time in John Hejduk's archive and relayed how much he appreciates the design of Adolf Loos's last house (Figure 1.22). He explained (emphasis ours[14]),

---

13   Stewart Hicks and Allison Newmeyer.
14   Stewart Hicks and Allison Newmeyer's.

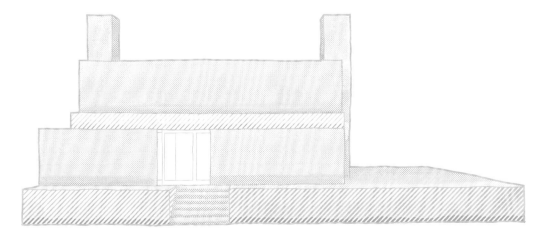

Figure 1.21: MOS Architects, Brick House. Illustration by Design With Company.

I[15] don't even know how to talk about this stuff really well, but let's say...the anthropomorphizing of architecture. Which I know some people have a really hard time with, and we do too, but we've been pushing ourselves to put things on the edge of, let's say, faces. That's why I liked that last house...by Adolf Loos. [It's] this funny house...I had never seen it before. ... Maybe I skipped over it. ...It's for sure [by] a guy who's ending life badly—[suffering] a diminished status in the field. ...It's a self-portrait. For me, there's no other way to look at it. It has a little mustache balustrade. ...Things that seem familiar or not, or abstraction and not abstraction—all of these things, I think, resonate with us still as kind of valid pleasures.

One night, when I[16] was about seven years old, my sister about three, I walked into our shared bedroom to find her sitting on the floor, in front of the room's one large window, sobbing. When I asked her what was wrong, she cried, "I'm afraid of the buildings!"

At the time, we[17] lived on the twenty-ninth floor of a high-rise in Hell's Kitchen, in Manhattan. The views from our windows consisted of steep vertical canyons, at the bottom of which you could faintly make out ant-like people and matchbox cars. At night, with their windows lit up yellow, the buildings across from us did in fact look sentient—as though they had many eyes, all of them watching us.

I knew this was what my[18] sister meant—that she felt the buildings were alive, that their eyes could see us. I tried to explain that there was nothing to be afraid of. But I probably wasn't very convincing. I was afraid of the buildings myself.

When I started writing fiction, I noticed that a certain feeling would come over me before I wrote something really good. I'm not talking about "inspiration," which is a word related to breath. I'm talking about something related to sight, but not sight exactly: a feeling of suddenly heightened perception, a sense that everything around me—including and especially the inanimate objects—was alive, sentient, and alert. It was as though by squinting just right,

15 Michael Meredith, Practice Architecture Talks (@practice_architecture_talks), "Talk No. 5," IGTV, Instagram, June 29, 2020, https://www.instagram.com/tv/CCCFAMSJwfx/.

16 Amy Bonnaffons.

17 Amy Bonnaffons and her family.

18 Amy Bonnaffons's.

Fig. 1.22: Adolf Loos, *The Last House*, 1932. Illustration by Design With Company.

I could tap into this vibrating layer of matter just below the surface, a layer that both invited and repelled my attention; it insisted on its own presence but resisted being fully known.

I believe it's this feeling that the Russian formalists were describing with the term *ostranenie*—estrangement, or defamiliarization. As Victor Shklovsky wrote: "The purpose of art is to impart the sensation of things as they are perceived and not as they are known. The technique of art is to make objects 'unfamiliar.'"[19] The idea was that great art takes ordinary things—the things we[20] barely see, because we take them so for granted—and forces us to recognize them as wild, strange, unknowable.

This feeling also may have been what the poet H. D. was describing in *Notes on Thought and Vision*:

> When a creative scientist, artist or philosopher has been for some hours or days intent on his work, his mind often takes on an almost physical character. That is, his mind becomes his real body. His over-mind becomes his brain. If I[21] could visualise or describe that over-mind in my own case, I should say this: it seems to me that it is a cap over my head, a cap of consciousness over my head, my forehead, affecting a little my
>
> eyes. Sometimes when I am in that state of consciousness, things about me appear slightly blurred as if seen under water. ...That over-mind seems a cap, like water, transparent, fluid yet with a definite body, contained in a definite space. It is like a closed sea-plant, jellyfish or anemone. Into that over-mind, thoughts pass and are visible like fish swimming under clear water.

H. D.'s "jellyfish"—a kind of translucent cap that fits over the mind and eyes, transforming perception by scrambling perception—feels like an accurate, if idiosyncratic, way to describe the feeling of estrangement that precedes good writing. If the trick of *ostranenie*, if the work of the jellyfish, is at least in part visual—if it depends in part upon eyes—then it is particularly interesting to examine descriptions of eyes that employ this estranging, defamiliarizing literary technique.

They can imagine the eye as inhabited or possessed, as in Arundhati Roy's *God of Small Things*: "So Small God laughed a hollow laugh. ...He climbed into people's eyes and became an exasperating expression."[22] Or as conscious and desiring, as in Ocean Vuong's *On Earth We're Briefly Gorgeous*: "You once told me that the human eye is god's loneliest creation. How so

19 Victor Shklovsky, "Art as Technique" (1917), in *Modernism: An Anthology of Sources and Documents*, ed. Jane Goldman et al. (Chicago: University of Chicago Press, 1998), 219.

20 The collective "we" of humanity.

21 H. D., *Notes on Thought and Vision* (San Francisco: City Lights Books, 1982).

22 Arundhati Roy, *The God of Small Things*, paperback ed. (New York: Random House Trade Paperbacks, 2008), 20.

much of the world passes through the pupil and still it holds nothing. The eye, alone in its socket, doesn't even know there's another one, just like it, an inch away, just as hungry, as empty."[23] Even the mysterious transparency of the eye itself can take on agency, as the embodiment of a character's emptiness or estrangement from self. This happens in Toni Morrison's *The Bluest Eye* ("She would never know her beauty. She would see only what there was to see: the eyes of other people")[24] and Edith Wharton's *The Age of Innocence* ("He shivered a little, remembering some of the new ideas in his scientific books, and the much-cited instance of the Kentucky cave-fish, which had ceased to develop eyes because they had no use for them. What if, when he had bidden May Welland to open hers, they could only look out blankly at blankness?").[25]

Such passages, in defamiliarizing the eye itself, ask us[26] to reconsider the ways in which sight is neither passive nor impartial. Yes, we watch the world around us—but we also watch others watching the world; we watch the world watching us, as my[27] sister did when she cried on the bedroom floor that night, feeling unsettlingly seen by eyes that she didn't know how to read. In our[28] watching, we hunger for something that the world seems to withhold.

But perhaps it's only when we perceive this withholding that we feel fully alert, in the way that *ostranenie* demands of us. In this state, we cannot reduce the world to fit our ideas of it. We cannot fantasize ourselves to be masters of the visible world. We feel ourselves willingly trapped in the snare of the present moment, primed for true encounter.

I[29] first noticed him at the bus stop one hot day in mid-August. He was hard not to notice. I'm not the kind of person to use the word "aura," but this man seemed to glow. Maybe it was a trick of his coloring: white-gold skin, golden-blond hair, green eyes that actually seemed to crackle electrically in certain lights. ...

I looked at him a lot. I touched him all over with the fingers of my eyes. Some men's handsomeness is a trick of the light and cannot survive such probing, but he held up. ...

During lulls in my workday, I would sometimes close my eyes and think of the man from the bus stop, imagine what it might feel like for those electric eyes to linger on my face and body. I didn't picture him touching me, just looking at me. Would some chemical reaction occur on the surface of my skin and work its way in, communicate something silent and profound?

---

23   Ocean Vuong, *On Earth We're Briefly Gorgeous* (New York: Penguin Press, 2019), 12.

24   Toni Morrison, *The Bluest Eye*, 1st international ed. (1970; repr., New York: Vintage, 2007), 46–47.

25   Edith Wharton, *The Age of Innocence* (1920; repr., New York: Premier Classics, 2009), 70.

26   The collective "we" of humanity.

27   Amy Bonnaffons's.

28   The collective "we" of humanity's.

29   Rachel in Amy Bonnaffons, *The Regrets* (New York: Little, Brown and Company, 2020), 67–70.

While we[30] often think of architectural glass as colorless and immaterial, I'd[31] like to point out that clear glass has a physical presence and a full complement of optical properties. Light passing through glass can be transmitted, reflected, refracted, or absorbed in different quantities. Surface treatments, coatings, and applied films alter these properties, exchanging transparency for translucency, specular for diffuse reflections, or full transmittance for selective reflectance. These treatments reveal the complexity of glass as a material, beyond transparency.

Dichroism is the material property of appearing to be two colors at once (Figure 1.23). Dichroic glass, which dates to Roman times, was originally made by adding gold and silver particles to the glass melt. Modern dichroic glass uses thin-film coatings—microscopic layers of metal oxide fused to the glass surface—to selectively reflect specific wavelengths of light, like an iridescent film of oil on water. Dichroic glass reflects one color and transmits another, the colors changing based on the angle of light and the angle of view.

These effects make glass that is transparent from one angle appear opaque from another—for example, reflecting gold while casting green shadows, as if the glass is glowing from within. This is not so much a "trick" of the light as a revelation of the inherent physical properties of glass, and the light, itself.

I[32] kept furtively staring at the woman directly across from me. …

I wasn't the only one staring. In fact, it seemed like everyone else in the room was either staring at her or trying very hard not to. By the way she carried

---

30 The collective "we" of architecture and humanity.
31 Gaby Brainard would.
32 The narrator in Amy Bonnaffons, "Goddess Night," in *The Wrong Heaven* (New York: Little, Brown and Company, 2018), 222.

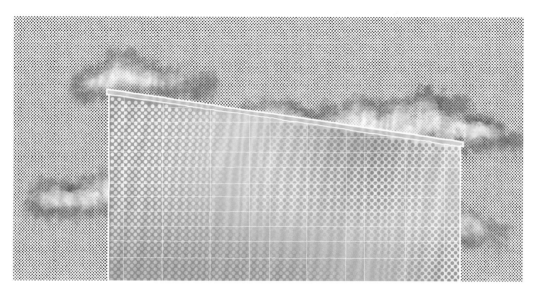

Figure 1.23: Dichroic glass facade. Illustration by Design With Company.

herself, you could tell she was used to being stared at, that not only was she comfortable in her own skin, but she also wore a second skin over her own, which consisted of people's stares, and she was comfortable in that too. When she moved—for example, raised her knee and rested an elbow on it—you could see her moving within this invisible cloak of stares, rearranging it around herself like a long flowing garment.

On its own, a single layer of glass is a poor insulator, but doubling it up improves its thermal performance and provides a number of secondary affects that I[33] appreciate. Storm or "double" windows, which date to the late seventeenth century,[34] were the original double-skin facade. Adding an additional layer of fixed glass outside of a building's "normal" windows in cold weather creates a buffer by trapping a layer of dead air, which is heated by the greenhouse effect. Today, storm windows have largely been replaced by "double-glazing," or insulated glazing units (IGUs)—a sealed, high-tech version of double windows reduced to one-inch thickness. Modern double-skin glass facades (DSFs) vary widely in structure and function, primarily depending on whether one or both lites open to the exterior or interior. Operable double-skin facades can provide thermal and acoustic buffering, natural ventilation, and varied modes of operation, from summer to winter or day to night. But letting in outside air introduces a host of undesirable elements—dust, dirt, pollution, humidity—and requires designers to provide for the cleaning and maintenance of all exposed glass surfaces.

Fully sealed double facades, known as closed-cavity facades (CCFs), have distinct advantages over operable double skins (Figure 1.24). The space between the two glass lites is factory-sealed, keeping out pollution and humidity, and is further ventilated with dry, filtered air to prevent condensation. With no requirements for access and cleaning, the cavity itself can be much thinner—often just the depth of the supporting mullion. The sealed airspace is an excellent location for automated blinds. If the outer lite is monolithic (single-layer) glass, these shades sit outside the thermal envelope—preventing solar gain while remaining protected from exterior wind and weather.

This opens up architectural possibilities. If solar gain is managed primarily through operable shading, the exterior, monolithic glass lite can remain uncoated, offering unparalleled transparency.[35] Such a facade might wrap a building like an "invisible cloak," enveloping it in a diaphanous membrane, a second skin that seems barely there.

---

33   Gaby Brainard.

34   Thomas Herzog, *Facade Construction Manual* (Basel: Birkhäuser, 2004), 233.

35   Uncoated, monolithic glass reflects 8 percent of visible light, while most low-e coatings (on IGUs) reflect 15 to 25 percent of visible light. See Viracon, http://www.viracon.com.

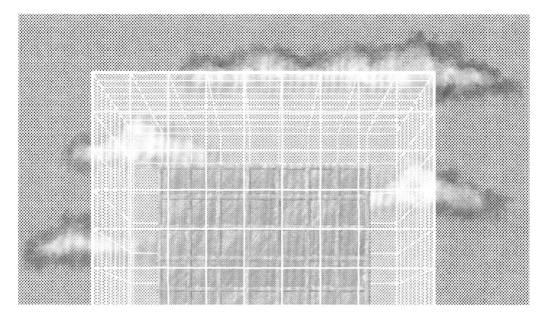

Figure 1.24: Closed-cavity facade. Illustration by Design With Company.

Recently I[36] began making videos for YouTube. Online teaching revealed just how little content there is out there that presents architectural design concepts to a broad audience. One of the early videos I made was on Le Corbusier's use of the "free" plan as it relates to the "organic" plans of Frank Lloyd Wright and the "open" plans of Ludwig Mies van der Rohe. During the video, I made a skit using a green screen that placed my head into the Villa Savoye at a scale where my eyes lined up with the ribbon window of the east facade. I delivered a speech from the vantage point of the Villa Savoye, arguing for the benefits of my[37] pilotis, windows, and so on. To date, this is the second-most-viewed video on the channel. I[38] suspect people can appreciate particular design decisions a little more when they no longer see the building as an inevitable, a priori occurrence.

"They had stared at her with great uncomprehending eyes. Eyes that questioned nothing and asked everything. <u>Unblinking and unabashed</u>, they stared up at her. <u>The end of the world lay in their eyes, and the beginning</u>, and all the waste in between."

"Only her tight, tight eyes were left. They were always left. ...

They were everything. Everything was there, in them. ...Thrown, in this way, into the binding conviction that only a miracle could relieve her, <u>she would never know her beauty. She would see only what there was to see: the eyes of other people</u>."

---

36   Stewart Hicks.
37   the Villa Savoye's.
38   Stewart Hicks.

"Someone appeared, with gentle and penetrating eyes, who—with no exchange of words—understood; and before whose glance...her eyes dropped. The someone had no face, no form, no voice, no odor. He was a simple Presence, an all-embracing tenderness with strength and a promise of rest."[39]

My[40] introduction to mirror glass was in the late 1980s, when I started seeing more and more on skyscrapers. Fredric Jameson described the mirrored

cylinders of John Portman's Bonaventure Hotel, in Los Angeles, as a "glass skin [that] repels the city outside," akin to wearing "reflector sunglasses."[41] For him, the mirrored facade dissociates and distorts the surrounding city while masking the building itself. The "unblinking" mirror, whose internal reflections contain whole worlds, prevents us—and others—from seeing ourselves.

Metaphor aside, neither writer considers the technical reasons for choosing

39   Morrison, *Bluest Eye*, 92, 45–47, 113.
40   Gaby Brainard's.
41   Fredric Jameson, *Postmodernism, or the Cultural Logic of Late Capitalism* (Durham, NC: Duke University Press, 1991), 42.

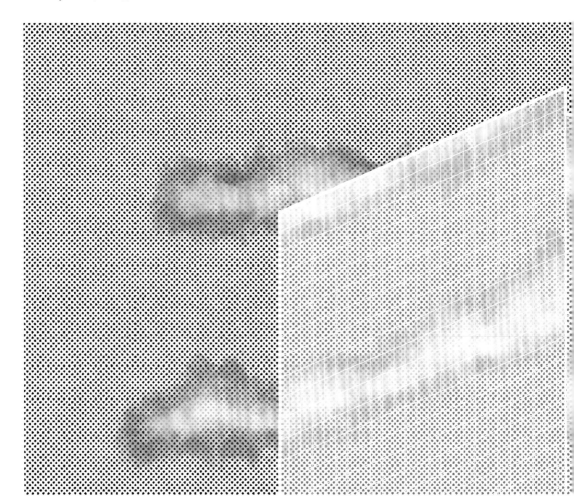

Figure 1.25: Mirrored facade. Illustration by Design With Company.

reflective glass in the 1980s. At the time, low-emissivity ("low-e") glass technology was dominated by the pyrolytic or "hard-coat" process, which produced highly reflective glass that was poor at blocking solar radiation.[42] Because the energy balance of commercial buildings is dominated by internal loads, reducing heat gain from sunlight is often a primary goal of glass selection. When solar-control low-e coatings produced by the magnetron sputter or "soft-coat" process were commercialized in the 1990s, architects flocked to these more transparent, less reflective coatings that delivered light without heat (Figure 1.25)

So why would an architect use mirror glass today, when most commercial architects seek out glass that is as transparent as possible? Consider Fumihiko Maki's 4 World Trade Center, an office tower in Lower Manhattan that resembles the abstract, prismatic forms of minimalist sculpture. The reflective glass is extremely flat, and rather than producing distorted reflections of the city, it reflects the sky, neighboring buildings, and adjacent World Trade Center memorial site faithfully. Indeed, the architect describes the building as morphing from a "sculptural object to one that blends and becomes a part of the sky." Perhaps reflectivity, as a considered aesthetic choice, can become a "quiet presence" in the city, projecting empathy for its context.[43]

We[44] trust that you will find this evidence intriguing. While we have not done a great job organizing it, the main connections and through lines remain largely intact. Architecture should recognize its emotional blind spot to building faces. We all see it except you. Some sort of Rorschach test is all we need to diagnose the problem more fully. Meanwhile, we have done quite well operating like therapists, offering a listening ear, and bonding with those who can see them too. Once we have the test, however, the experts can take it from there. ●

42   These products, known as "passive low-e," have solar heat gain coefficients in the 0.45–0.66 range, versus 0.27–0.30 (or lower) for triple-silver low-e sputter coatings. http://glassed.vitroglazings.com/topics/how-low-e-glass-works.

43   "4 World Trade Center," Maki and Associates, accessed April 26, 2021, http://www.maki-and-associates.co.jp/details/index_pic.html?pcd=95.

44   Stewart Hicks and Allison Newmeyer.

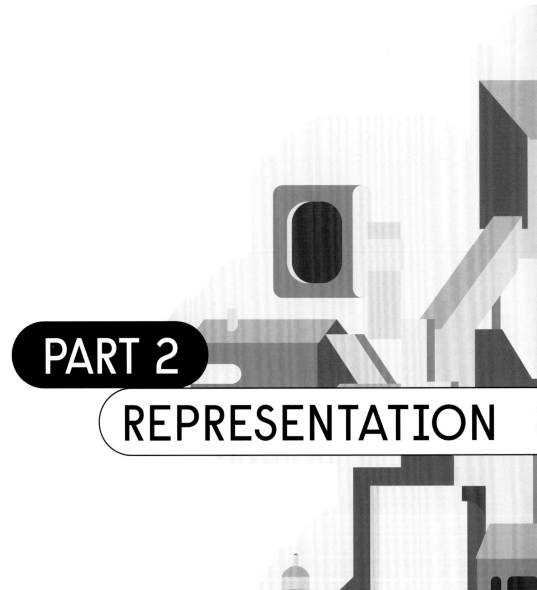

PART 2

REPRESENTATION

& CITIZENSHIP

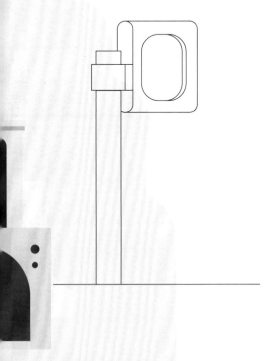

Of the Present

From the Occuli of the Tower

It was a rainy night in Chicago. The streets were even quieter than they usually are during a rainstorm. The world was several weeks into a pandemic; people in the city (and all over the globe) were hunkered down in their homes, quarantined for safety, and I was empty. My lobby, elevators, hallways, and offices were somber, dead spaces, irrelevant in this new reality.

On most days I felt useless, but on this night I was also scared for my own safety. The storm was one of the worst I've seen in the forty-seven years since I turned my lights on for the first time. I've been through some bad ones, but I knew from the start that this was a doozy. The rain was heavy and relentless. Torrents of runoff rushed down Wacker Drive. By midnight the floodwater on Lower Wacker seeped into my basement and created deep pud-

dles that soon became a rapidly rising pool. By 2 a.m. the
water overwhelmed my substation. I lost all power, and
my lights went out.

I stood there exposed, without the mask of my twinkling
illuminated windows. I was a pitch-black monolith tower-
ing above the city, with no way to disguise my disappointment, my humiliation, my shame, my fear. It was written
all over my face. I was supposed to be your heroic skyscraper, your symbol of strength, hope, and the American
way, your broad shoulders. But now I was a looming menace, a reminder of your mistakes and of the consequences
yet to come. I am certainly no hero. I am just a building...a
creaturely building, vulnerable and flawed.

From a Mind in the Gutter

Lately, you only love me for my walls.

For two months, you barely even opened my doors and windows, except to occasionally retrieve lukewarm but aromatic brown paper bags that strangers would periodically drop on my concrete stoop. You used to make better use of my orifices. My porch and vestibule were heavily trafficked, welcoming your brothers, sisters, and friends in and out of my well-tempered interior. I took pride in ushering them in from a spring storm through my squeaky front door. I giggled when your guests fumbled on the stairwell and danced around one another to maneuver the removal of their shoes on the narrow landing. Their inadvertent caresses made me blush.

You and I have been intimately close for several years, and I genuinely appreciate your companionship, but I'm confused about why you no longer leave my side. You seem extra fond of your bed, a companion platform to my creaky floors that was once reserved for rest and sometimes romance. Now you use it to exercise, eat, and talk to your coworkers on a screen for many hours on end. I used to see you step out of the bedroom in the morning with an energetic bounce; now this room seems to perpetuate your stasis and fatigue. I suspect a little time apart might be healthy for both of us.

You don't often talk to me directly, but when you do, all I hear is complaints. "Why are you so drafty?" you lament at my front windows. "Why can't you have more space?" you wonder aloud as your two children run laps between my two ends. "Where is that sound coming from?" you cry when I flex my woody sinews throughout my framing. During the torrential downpour last night, I redirected gallons and gallons of frigid precipitation off my roof into my gutters and discharged dramatically from my scuppers. My robust capacity to shed moisture can go only so far without a little help from you. Instead of appreciating my diligent efforts toward maintaining your comfort, you screamed in disgust when a small leak sprung from a scrappy corner of my living room ceiling, beneath an overextended patch of my ridged roof. Should I really be held accountable for this body's imperfect physique when I can barely call it my own? ●

Animism, or How Architectural Creatures Locomote

Did you see that? That *building* just walked—further than I've walked during this entire pandemic!

—Trevor Noah

Animation is a term that differs from, but is often confused with, motion. Where motion implies movement and action, anima-tion...suggests animalism, animism, growth, actuation, vitality and virtuality.

—Greg Lynn

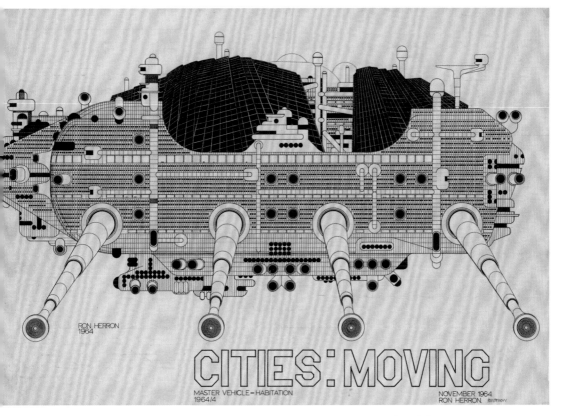

Figure 2.1. Ron Herron, *Walking City*, 1964. Digital Image © The Museum of Modern Art, Licensed by SCALA / Art Resource, NY and Artist Rights Society (ARS).

WALKING BUILDINGS

In an October 2020 segment of *The Daily Show*, Trevor Noah responds to a news story about a historic building in Shanghai outfitted with robotic legs that allowed it to walk more than two hundred feet, making way for the construction of a new skyscraper and avoiding demolition.

Noah cracks a full spectrum of jokes about the building's locomotion, invoking emotional irony ("what a great moment this is for the architect, because it's always special to see your building take its first steps"), scatological slapstick ("I just feel bad for the guy who was using the bathroom while this was happening"), practical skepticism ("I don't want to go all the way down to the DMV and then find out that it's on vacation in the Hamptons"), and projective imagination for an antiracist city ("walking buildings might be the only way to avoid gentrification").[1] The range of responses elicited by the walking building, from serious to silly and from practical to political, point to an augmented agency granted to buildings liberated from their traditionally fixed foundations. Like

---

1 *The Daily Show with Trevor Noah*, "Obama Roasts Trump & Pope Francis Approves Same Sex Civil Unions," October 23, 2020, video, 9:17, https://www.youtube.com/watch?v=d3xLm7XLCh4.

most good comedy, the humor Noah finds in this absurd image is derived from several mundane truths about our relationship to architecture, including our assumption that buildings are meant to stay in one place in order to provide us with privacy, protection, and good neighborly relationships. And yet Noah also sees the potential benefits of a self-propelled building. One possible superpower of architecture is the ability to bring forth a future where buildings provide a different set of affordances beyond what our current conditions require, especially an architecture with this type of enhanced agency (e.g., evading gentrification).

Noah also senses that architects see buildings as more than inert objects with a predetermined existence—perhaps we do see them as our babies. We conceive them through collaborative engagement with clients and other design professionals (or simply our own imaginations); we gestate them through schematic drawings and detailed instructions to builders. And after we give birth, we hold our breath and hope that they will survive, thrive, and continue to grow and develop through their interactions with the big, wide world. In some sense, the buildings that architects design are more real in their imaginations, or in their drawings, than they are in built form, which is perhaps one of the reasons that architects simultaneously frustrate and fascinate the rest of the world.

It is also the reason that walking buildings are something that architects have already imagined in the context of speculative projects. While some architects use drawings as a means to an end (to produce a building), others see drawing as an end in itself, as a way to test ideas about architecture that would be far-fetched to build or that challenge the certainty of our current reality. Yet in all the ways that architects use drawings, even in mundane house plans, there is an implicit magic: an ability to conjure a new thing into being, even if only by virtue of our imaginations (kind of like the cave paintings at Lascaux). If seeing is believing, then the conventions of architectural drawing follow a logic and precision that can produce the effect of plausibility, allowing us to see something's potential to come to life, regardless of whether our rational minds initially accept it. For this reason, it is not outrageous to suggest that many, if not most, architects are actually closet animists, even if they are not aware of it themselves. It is the purpose of this essay to expose and explore this latent animism by looking at projects that already swim openly in or close to animist waters, and then by understanding what both architects and their audiences have to gain by diving in the deep end.

WALKING CITIES AND WAKING MOUNTAINS

> That inanimate objects and things act, that they have designs on us, and that we are interpellated by them, is a quotidian reality that we all implicitly accept—just as we accept, and indeed are animated by, the very milieus and contexts in which we operate. But to acknowledge, articulate, and conceptualize this fact is apparently a wholly different issue. ...Imagining animism therefore takes on the shape of the extreme, such that animism assumes the form of a caricature-version of the reality we normally take for granted: If things become active, alive, or even person-like, where does that leave actual humans?
>
> —Anselm Franke[2]

In this book's first essay, we outlined the contribution of zoomorphism to the production of architectural creatures with formal characteristics of animate beings. In the second essay, we pivot our attention to speculate on the relationship between animist architecture and our notion of a creaturely human subjectivity. Whereas zoomorphic architecture suggests a building that resembles an animal, animist architecture attributes an animal-like liveliness and animation to buildings, cultivating a new kind of relational awareness in human occupants and companions. Animism suggests the agency to move like an animal or to affect change through the motion and power of one's body, among other lively qualities. Locomotion, or the capacity to move around the world, is perhaps the most explicit expression of an animist architecture that challenges human assumptions about our relationship to the built environment and how we define ideas about place, home, our bodies and our sense of belonging. By disrupting these assumptions, locomoting buildings offer a chance to revise these definitions, and in turn expand the ways that architecture supports our interactions with and relationships to other beings.

Archigram's *Walking City* (1964) is a canonical example of peripatetic architecture that flaunts its literal mobility (Figure 2.1). This speculative project imagines families of mobile megastructures that house "a large population of world traveler-workers" as they slowly migrate across a dystopian earth.[3] Each megastructure unit resembles a mash-up of a submarine and an insect (or arachnid?), with four pairs of slender, telescoping legs that elevate its densely populated thorax 180 feet above the ground and empower it to traverse surf and turf, including derelict cityscapes and barren dunescapes. Retractable corridor tubes enable multiple walking city units to link up with one another to exchange resources, inhabitants, and information. *Walking City* exaggerates and delivers the capacity for buildings

2   Anselm Franke, "Animism: Notes on an Exhibition," *e-flux journal* 36 (July 2012), https://www.e-flux.com/journal/36/61258/animism-notes-on-an-exhibition/.

3   Warren Chalk, Peter Cook, Dennis Crompton, David Greene, Ron Herron, and Michael Webb, *Archigram: The Book* (London: Circa Press, 2018), 104.

not only to locomote across the planet, but also to dynamically connect to and disconnect from one another in ongoing hookups and productive couplings. In Archigram's vision of the world, architecture behaves emphatically like a creeping organism in an ever-changing relationship to other organisms and environments. Despite the project's reliance on advanced technologies, the image of *Walking City*'s mountain-sized megastructures moving across the landscape conjures the mythic creatures mentioned earlier in this book, Acheron, the Kami, and Turtle Island, whose enormous scale enables them to house thousands of humans, an archipelago, or a continent. In the northeastern United States, the Mohican and Lenape Nations describe the formation of the Catskill Mountains as the fallen body of a great monster, Ontiora (Sky Mountains), who was slain by Manitou (Great Mystery).[4] Interpreted through this story, the megastructures of *Walking City* might be imagined as the bodies of mountains that have come back to life to walk the earth once again. While there is a certain dissonance between the Western worldview that produced Archigram's techno-dystopian fantasy and the Indigenous worldview that understands landforms as animate matter, this reading of Ontiora as an unacknowledged precedent of *Walking City* also helps to dispel the anti-animist assumptions embedded in Western thought.

---

4   Thursty McQuill, *The Hudson River by Daylight: New York to Albany and Troy* (New York: Bryant Literary Union, 1884), 60-61.

Figure 2.2. Shin Yoshiwara ōnamazu yurai. Wikimedia Commons.

Nevertheless, in order to properly credit any subliminal Indigenous influence on instances of Western animism, we must first confront the white-supremacist/Eurocentric origins of the term. As the German curator Anselm Franke writes, the nineteenth-century anthropologist Edward Tylor coined the term animism to describe the "primordial mistake of primitive people who attributed life and person-like qualities to objects in their environment."[5] This definition allowed Tylor and his colleagues to draw a distinct line between so-called "primitive" and "civilized" cultures by using this "mistake" to fabricate an evolutionary hierarchy within the human family, one with modern European cultures located on top.[6] Given the term's origin in and deep ties to the colonialist project, certain contemporary scholars avoid it altogether. However, other scholars, including Irving Hallowell, Nurit Bird-David, Te Pakaka Tawhai, and Graham Harvey, have reclaimed the term as part of a "new animism" and "as a shorthand reference to their efforts to re-imagine and redirect human participation in the larger-than-human, multi-species community," as Harvey describes.[7] This updated conceptualization takes seriously the cultural practices of animism that represent a worldview based on relational forms of knowledge, rejecting modernity's dualistic perspective defined by rigid distinctions between life and non-life, human and nonhuman, subject and object, nature and culture.[8]

Furthermore, contemporary philosophers, political theorists, educators, and artists are leveraging the perspective of the new animism to critique the anthropocentric, colonialist traditions of Western disciplines from the inside out. Timothy Morton decenters humans from Marxist theory in the name of ecological solidarity, claiming that "Marxism only works if it weirdly embraces animism."[9] Morton's version of ecological thought requires that we learn to see and think of things—whether human, animal, plant, or weather system—as neither alive nor dead, but as *spectral*, a quality defined by a kind of shimmering and flickering of quantum movement and overlapping relational coexistence. Jane Bennett defines a *vital materialism* through the "traces of independence or aliveness" manifested by "the thing formerly known as an object."[10] Jane Merewether corrects Jean Piaget's classification of children's animism as a "primitive" stage in development that is outgrown once they reach "a more advanced and

5   Anselm Franke, "Much Trouble in the Transportation of Souls, or The Sudden Disorganization of Boundaries," in *Animism, Volume 1*, ed. Anselm Franke (Berlin: Sternberg Press: 2010), 11–12.

6   See Jane Merewether, "Enchanted Animism: A Matter of Care," *Contemporary Issues in Early Childhood* (November 2020): 2, https://doi.org/10.1177%2F1463949120971380.

7   Graham Harvey, introduction to *The Handbook of Contemporary Animism*, ed. Graham Harvey (New York: Routledge, 2013), 2.

8   For more on dualism in Western culture, along with a list of references to scholars who have engaged it, see Priscilla Stuckey, "The Animal versus the Social: Rethinking Individual and Community in Western Cosmology," in Harvey, *Handbook of Contemporary Animism*, 192.

9   Timothy Morton, *Humankind: Solidarity with Nonhuman People* (Brooklyn: Verso, 2017), 97.

10 Jane Bennett, *Vibrant Matter: A Political Ecology of Things* (Durham, NC: Duke University Press, 2010), xvi.

'rational' stage."[11] Instead, her enchanted animism is a speculative playfulness that draws on Maria Puig de la Bellacasa's definition of the speculative as "a mode of thought committed to foster visions of other worlds possible."[12] These contemporary thinkers provide an opportunity to locate the animate qualities of architecture in a broader ontological context that dismantles the hegemony of human privilege. As Franke points out above, we actually do accept, and even take for granted, the agency and impact that "inanimate objects" have in our lives. Yet to actively acknowledge and articulate this animist fact as a defining characteristic of our Western worldview is to render a seemingly caricature-like version of the more inert reality we are conditioned to perceive. While the commonplace and sometimes invisible motion of building parts normalizes certain categories of movement as part of a building's typical "behavior," we don't often take seriously the capacity for architecture to locomote. Even while we are aware of the living qualities of the architectures we inhabit, an actual walking building in Shanghai appears absurdly cartoonish to our eyes.

In the Eurocentric tradition, architecture is both conceptualized and constructed as a fixed, static, and permanent entity that is literally or figuratively planted in the ground. In turn, this "groundedness" suggests a structural stability, moral integrity, and material and cultural permanence. As Victor Hugo famously mused in *The Hunchback of Notre-Dame*, "Architecture has recorded the great ideas of the human race. Not only every religious symbol, but every human thought has its page in that vast book."[13] For Hugo, only the book itself, and its capacity to be printed and disseminated en masse, can threaten architecture's role as the preeminent, eternal index of human culture ("this will kill that"). But architecture is not fixed, static, or permanent. Buildings get lived in, cluttered, and soiled. As Hugo may have anticipated with dread, cathedrals burn and museums are demolished. Small buildings are renovated, remodeled, and added onto—or sometimes even relocated to a new plot of land altogether, as Trevor Noah comically recounts.

Short of changing addresses, buildings can move in a variety of other familiar ways—structurally and technologically as well as functionally and poetically. From simple operable windows to automated kinetic facades, from quotidian garage doors to spectacular retractable roofs on stadiums, and from glass elevators to revolving rooftop restaurants, buildings have featured moving parts among their assemblages of components for centuries. And while most well-engineered buildings feel relatively static as we walk around in them, the structural elements that keep buildings standing up and stable are subject to both the fixed "dead loads" of the materials themselves and the constantly

---

11   Merewether, "Enchanted Animism," 1.

12   Quoted in Merewether, 4.

13   Victor Hugo, *The Hunchback of Notre-Dame* (1831; trans. 1879; repr., New York: Tom Doherty Associates, 1996), 162.

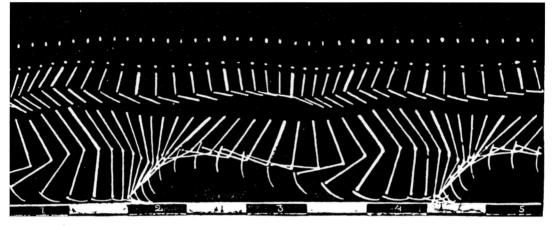

Figure 2.3. Étienne-Jules Marey, *Positions of the Extremities of the Soldier During Double Time.* Wikimedia Commons.

changing "live loads" of moving people, stuff, and weather events, which exert physical forces that cause the ongoing expansion and contraction of a building's materials. Just as the term "live loads" implies living actants pushing and pulling on a building's anatomy, so too it summons a building's lineaments to come to life, to react reflexively to avoid structural failure. When you hear the floorboards creak beneath your strolling feet, the building is signaling its active movement in response to your distinctive gait.[14] If Morton had his way, "live" and "dead" loads might be called "spectral loads" instead.

Moreover, because architecture is a container for people and activities, the potential energy for buildings to locomote is necessarily bound up with the behavioral habits and circulation patterns of the locomoting humans and nonhumans who inhabit them, as well as the ecological contexts in which they are located. Given this awareness, it is both impossible to write off any building as a static, inert, lifeless object and tempting to describe it as possessing some kind of life of its own. Bennett's theory of vital materialism not only identifies "thing-power," which "aims to attend to the it as an actant...and to name the moment of independence (from subjectivity) possessed by things,"[15] but also makes the case for a new grammar of agency that accounts for the "collaboration, cooperation, or interactive interference" that occurs in human-nonhuman assemblages (as opposed to the default assumption of active people and passive objects). Similarly, Morton seeks to "soften the edges between 'act' and 'behave'": "'To act' and 'to behave' need to be seen as dual aspects of one being. They slide over one another, generating a spectral, breathing nowness."[16] In both instances, the endowment of agency to nonhuman or abiotic entities is less about empowering them with a will to act equivalent to that of humans, and more about reframing and reducing the

---

14   See Franz Kafka's short story "The Bridge," which relays the structural life and death of a footbridge in the first person.

15   Bennett, *Vibrant Matter*, 3, 21.

16   Morton, *Humankind*, 81.

Figure 2.4. Thomas Thwaites, Goat Man, 2016. Photo by Tim Bowditch. Thwaites designed a set of prosthetic limbs that allowed him to walk on four legs in the posture of a goat.

self-importance of human's perceived agency as a unique and all-powerful force in the universe. Both scholars relocate and redistribute agency within the context of an ecological symbiosis with all other beings, which easily includes buildings and other designed elements of our environments.

Morton and Bennett identify the source of this vital or shimmering quality of all things in the fact that their existence, identities, and expressions are defined by a fuzzy boundary that allows for and depends on intimate relationships to other things. If we understand a human being to be dependent on the microorganisms within their intestinal biome and the weather systems that are responsible for their food system, how can we draw a clear line around a single unit of the human species? The same interdependence applies to the aggregation of materials, infrastructures, forces, biotic inhabitants, activities, thermodynamics, and so on that compose a building. In both cases, our perception of humans as a singular source of action or agency is called into question, and in this space of uncertainty, an animist perspective promotes a new speculative potential. When ideas of animism challenge architecture's traditionally rooted relationship to the ground in order to initiate opportunities for literal mobility, fictional motion, and animated behavior more broadly, they also refigure the role of human occupants within that new context.

THE PACK DONKEY'S PLAN

> When my ancestor on the East African savanna hoisted herself for the first time onto her hind legs, it was a journey of far more than a few feet. It was a journey into a new world. She was immediately a creature whose world was framed not by the top of the grass and the baked mud of the ground, but by the far horizon and the stars. The Genesis account was suddenly true: she had visual dominion over the things that crept and crawled. She saw them in a way that they did not see her: they looked up to her, and she couldn't help looking down on them. ...She saw their backs, their contexts, and the patterns of their lives.
>
> —Charles Foster[17]

It is one thing to expand our human worldview to welcome a wider range of nonhuman beings and things into our once-exclusive realm of companionship and agency. It is quite another to allow our ecologically intimate interactions to change our worldview to the point that we can see things from the perspectives of other types of beings. Recent books like *GoatMan: How I Took a Holiday from Being Human*, by Thomas Thwaites, and *Being a Beast: Adventures Across the Species Divide*, by Charles Foster, recount and reflect on attempts by the authors to do just that—to live life from the point of view of another species. Thwaites designed a set of prosthetic limbs that allowed him to walk on four legs in the posture of a goat and an external stomach that digested grass on his behalf and then lived with goats on a farm in the Alps for several days (Figure 29). In contrast, Foster spent weeks at a time living without the aid of technology, and sometimes without clothing, in the habitats of five different species of animals native to the United Kingdom (badger, deer, otter, fox, and swift), equipped only with knowledge of their dietary and migratory habits and circadian rhythms and as much information as neuroscience had to offer about their means of processing sensory input from their environments. As a badger, he clawed his way through soil, lived in an underground burrow, and tried to rely more on his sense of smell than his eyesight when searching for food. As an otter, he spent days in the water fishing for trout with his teeth. As a swift, he never learned to fly. And while he readily admits that his failures were greater than his triumphs, in his writing he is able to close the gaps in his experience through his very human tools of philosophy and language. With these tools he was able to make the imaginative leaps that his body and neurology could not. We may attempt to make similar leaps with architecture and its distinctive disciplinary tools, as we shift our attention from architectural creatures (that look like nonhumans) to the ways that creaturely architecture can help to construct a more creaturely human subject.

---

17   Charles Foster, *Being a Beast: Adventures Across the Species Divide* (New York: Metropolitan Books, 2016), 17.

Whereas architectural zoomorphism tends to express itself in elevation and section, the logic of locomotion has a particular affiliation with architectural plans, the orthographic projection that highlights relationships between spatial organization and circulation patterns by abstracting a view of the world from above (or the upright perspective described by Charles Foster). Le Corbusier asserted his reverence for modern rational (top-down) planning by declaring plan drawings to be the generative force in architectural design. He simultaneously expressed his disdain for the chaotic, irregular geometries of the premodern city, which to his mind were a product of the pack donkey's wandering way. For us, that meandering figural line that he attributes to the donkey is not a sign of chaos, but of a different way of seeing, tracing, and moving through the world. Put another way, creatures don't usually walk around in routes that follow sharp right angles. A locomotive, creaturely architecture embraces the nonrational through its privileging of figural form over geometric order, specifically in plan.

Plan has a reputation as the strong and silent type. It usually plays its role out of sight and out of mind, imposing organizational authority on us at the volume of a whisper or as a subliminal command that operates on both the body and the unconscious. Sections and elevations tend to "speak" louder than plans—they communicate through visual cues, like shape, volume, light, material, and color, that are immediately accessible to human perception. Conversely, plans often communicate through tactics that are not always perceived consciously through sensory stimuli. Plans establish organizational structures, circulation patterns, programmatic sequences, and contextual relationships that inhabitants understand by processing layers of perception, engagement, and experience. Through this accumulation of sensory and cognitive input, the plan helps to construct a narrative, one which ultimately positions the human subject within the story of an architecture.

Conventionally, orthographic plan drawings are cut four feet above and parallel to the ground plane, an approach keyed to the upright human body. But what if we are interested in inserting a creaturely subject into the story of architecture? To consider this question, we look at approaches to drawing that leave behind the rationality of orthographic projection and the abstraction of the conventional plan in favor of other modes. Techniques that precisely tweak these conventions can present alternatives to this default "right-side-up" orientation by constructing environments that reorient our locomotion and relationship to the ground in ways that simulate how airborne, subterranean, or sticky-footed creatures inhabit the world. With creatures that occupy the dimensions of space through a range of relationships to ground, sky, gravity, and topology, the relationships conveyed by the horizontal orthographic view of a plan cut may be translated into the vertical orthographic view of a section cut (and vice versa). When one can crawl as easily along the wall as the floor, plan and section become interchangeable.

Axonometric, oblique, and perspective projections are drawing techniques that integrate information from plan, section, and elevation into a single drawing to convey a simulation of three-dimensional spatial experience, and therefore can be leveraged to communicate the alternative spatial orientations of nonhuman creatures. Three examples of recent speculative architecture projects generate creaturely spatial experiences by manipulating or leveraging drawing techniques that reference worm's-eye, bird's-eye, and tick's-eye vantage points, and prompt us to suspend our human assumptions of uprightness in order to enter the fictional world of the creature.

Bureau Spectacular's *Pool Party*, an installation proposed as an entry to MoMA PS1's Young Architects Program, simulates the experience of being inside a worm's-eye perspective drawing, casting human occupants into the role of virtual earthworms wriggling through an invisible stratum of soil beneath a collection of swimming pools (Figure 2.5). The project replaces the ground that swimming pools are typically embedded in with a diaphanous structural grid that elevates the basins high in the air. The high concrete walls that line the courtyard reinforce the fiction that the audience is exploring a subterranean world. While it doesn't presume that its audience is familiar with the architectural convention of the worm's-eye drawing, the project leverages lessons from the drawing technique to create a spatial experience that asks its inhabitants to reconsider the planes of human creaturely occupation and perception that we frequently take for grant-ed. The actual plan drawing for the project reinforces these spatial qualities by emphasizing the overlapping layers of pool figures, from those suspended in the air to those projected on the ground. The plan doesn't define boundaries and

Figure 2.5. Bureau Spectacular, *Pool Party*, 2017.

pathways along a single plane as much as it describes densities, opacities, and transparencies as they are experienced in three-dimensional space, in the same way that an earthworm moves through soil not from one floor plate to the next, but through a continuous, earthy matrix of variable porosities, water content, and mineral compositions that stretch out in both horizontal and vertical dimensions. For creatures that move like earthworms, the orientation of plan seamlessly transitions into section and vice versa, with little regard for gravity. In the world of *Pool Party*, humans have an opportunity to imagine themselves wiggling through a different kind of layered spatial construction.

Florencia Pita and Jackilin Hah Bloom's *New Zocalo*, a proposal for a public platform in Detroit exhibited at the 2016 Venice Architecture Biennale, challenges the conventional construction of human subjectivity by offering something akin to a bird's-eye view (Figure 2.6). A bird's-eye view is similar to a true plan; both share a

Figure 2.6. Florencia Pita and Jackilin Hah Bloom, *New Zocalo*, 2016.

Figure 2.7. Design With Company, *Collider Activity Center*, 2013.

vantage point from above. However, a bird also experiences a continuously shifting perspective as it takes off, transitions from vertical to horizontal motion, and returns to the ground, a tree, or a roof. In this way, its relationships to figure and ground are always changing—at one moment a building's elevation looms above, while at another moment the building's roof is ground, or the elevation drifts by alongside as it flies down the street. *New Zocalo* samples the hexagonal pattern of triangular blocks from August Woodward's 1805 master plan for Detroit and transposes them to become graphic pedestrian pathways and paving textures atop a civic plinth. Additional sampling generates the forms of buildings on the plinth, where profiles from structures in the surrounding neighborhood are cross-extruded to generate intricate new geometry and shapely landscaping. By physically treading on these familiar fragments in plan as opposed to viewing them elevationally, as in a drawing positioned on a wall, the content becomes experiential rather than interpretative. The fragments cannot be readily dissected, classified, or analyzed, but as a series of overlapping ground figures, they become a living diagram suggesting other ways to occupy the ground. The project operates like an occupiable map of a fictional cityscape. Unlike a GPS that directs you along an efficient, orthogonal path to reach a fixed endpoint, however, this map exposes the construction and logics of possible pathways to discover new and open-ended routes, while revealing that the urban ground itself (a plinth after all!) is a fabrication of the imagination.

Design With Company's *Collider Activity Center* generates a world that visitors experience like a tick nestled on a deer's body, where the relative "ground" fluctuates as humans climb across the architecture's vertical and canted recreational surfaces. As the headquarters for a rock-climbing company, the entire project serves as a demonstration of alternative forms of human engagement with ground, the surface on which we locomote and from which we orient ourselves to the rest of the world, whether horizontal, vertical, or somewhere in between. Most literally, this strategy includes climbing walls on the exterior skins of the buildings and on the perimeter wall. Even the most straightforward inhabitation of the horizontal ground plane is translated into a locomotive adventure that is narrated by the plan drawing, specifically the figural pedestrian track that circumscribes the site

Figure 2.8. Design With Company, *Collider Activity Center*, 2013.

(Figure 2.7). On one end, the track rises above the ground as an elevated walk-
way, while on the other, it twists and meanders at grade. For a pedestrian walking
or jogging on the track, the experience provides an ever-changing perspective
and relationship to the ground, setting up a scene in which bodies and buildings
cohabitate the campus loop (Figure 2.8). Each building is a character with personality and presence of its own, defined by a uniquely expressive silhouette with
idiosyncratic features composed of architectural elements—a leggy colonnade,
a coiffed sawtooth roofline, an oversized heady gable. As creatures in their own
rights, the buildings are spaced and oriented in relationship to one another not just
as a matter of plan organization, but as a form of plan-based storytelling. The site
plan determines who will face each other and at what proximity—it suggests which
buildings are friends and which are enemies, conditional relationships determined
by the interplay of the fixed footprint of the structures and the constantly changing
perspective of the viewer. As a human cohabitant moves around the track, their

view of the creature buildings is always locomoting—brushing up against an underbelly; spotting a pink head peeking out, ready to spy; or seeing, after rounding a corner, that the pink head is too preoccupied to spy on anyone because she is kissing the green-peaked griffin. On the far side of the track, humans are no longer companions to the crew of creatures, but rather observers, watching as they move together and apart, like characters in the fickle love stories of a tawdry telenovela.

Le Corbusier insistence on a superior human perspective is asserted via a literal top-down plan view, as seen from the upright human perspective. From this privileged vantage point, he imposes a view of his preferred orthogonal movement patterns of the modern city in order to reinforce the belief that we are different from the other animals. Rather than seeing to believe, the three projects discussed above help us to believe in our creaturely nature in order to see the world differently. Each constructs a unique spatial experience that offers a simulation of movement akin to that of various creatures. Through such movement we begin to believe in our own belonging to the greater creaturely community, and learn to see the rest of the world through this lens of creaturely camaraderie. The augmented plans of these projects reflect this alternative view of the world, not from the top down perspective of the human, but along the meandering path of the donkey.

ANIMIST ARCHITECTURE PRACTICES

Within the context of this animist ecological awareness, there are many possible trajectories for architectural investigation, especially in the realm of speculative projects that use drawings, models, books, and installations to explore experimental ideas. In his 1999 book *Animate Form*, Greg Lynn introduced the use of digital animation software as a novel tool that could integrate the forces, flows, and fields of motion that act upon an architectural object into the design of its form. For Lynn, this new process liberated architecture from traditional assumptions of its stasis and permanence to promote a new "ethics of motion" in form-making. The intention of Lynn's alternative ethics was to generate a set of flexible, mutable, and differential "expressions" of form, an approach that positions architecture "as a participant immersed within dynamical flows." In this context, Lynn makes a distinction between "actual" and "virtual" movement, arguing that virtual movement originates from within the architecture itself, as opposed to being a scenic effect that is registered around the architecture by a moving human viewer.[18] His canonical *Embryological House* applies these form-generating techniques based on virtual movement to the design of a manufactured home via a set of parameters adjusted according to contextual constraints to produce virtually unlimited iterations from an original "primitive." The result is a family of "genetically" similar forms, each an organism shaped in response to its unique conditions—an early

18   Greg Lynn, *Animate Form* (New York: Princeton Architectural Press, 1999), 25, 11, 10.

experiment in mass-customization (Figure 2.9). Viewed together, the collection conveys the sense of growth, development, distortion, and vitality generated as parameters shift from one house to the next. And yet, as a stand-alone form, a single house still reads as an autonomous object, a frozen snapshot of the context that formed it, with little continued sense of engagement or relationality with the biotic and abiotic flows and pulses in and around it.

As a contemporary of Lynn's influential text, the Tokyo-based practice Atelier Bow-Wow's 2001 publication *Made in Tokyo* shares an interest in the contextual flows and forces that shape architecture, but explores them from a very different perspective. The book documents existing urban structures that the authors refer to as "environmental units" because they blur boundaries between building, infrastructure, landscape, and city and demonstrate surprising and serendipitous juxtapositions of programs, activities, and types.[19] While the structures reflect more conventional form-making strategies, these unconventional juxtapositions

---

19   Momoyo Kaijima, Junzo Kuroda, and Yoshiharu Tsukamoto, *Made in Tokyo* (Tokyo: Kajima Institute Publishing, 2001), 11.

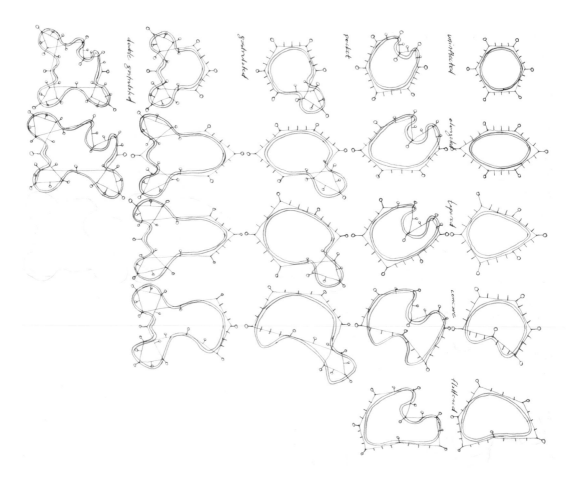

Figure 2.9. Greg Lynn, Sketches for *Embryological House*, 2000. Canadian Centre for Architecture, Gift of Greg Lynn © Greg Lynn.

complicate their reading as single building enclosures with clear distinctions between public and private, inside and outside, shallow and deep, back and front.
It is through these observations that Atelier Bow-Wow develops the concept of
"pet architecture" in *Made in Tokyo* and subsequent publications, proposing the
idea that like nonhuman companions, small buildings and urban objects hold a
subjective position in relation to the rest of the city and the people in it; that
is, buildings interact with other buildings, and buildings interact with people to
define new social configurations in the city. Objects such as vending machines,
karaoke boxes, parking lot kiosks, and signboards are described as pet-size: too
small to be architecture and too big to be furniture, they occupy a corner of a
room or a city and "[turn] the urban environment into a 'superinterior.'" These
objects are "a size which allows a freedom in urban action," "as an interface
between the city and the human body."[20] Atelier Bow-Wow's principals, Momoyo
Kaijima and Yoshiharu Tsukamoto, take the lessons learned from found objects
in the city as an opportunity to manipulate everyday objects to reveal new
meanings. They use the term "monsteration" to describe the "enlargement of
everyday things to make visible their distinctive values, producing shapes that
invoke monsters lurking within reality."[21]

Bureau Spectacular's early work advanced the spirit of Atelier Bow-Wow's re-
search-based urban concepts through the medium of comic-book stories that
speculate on the future of architecture, as well as installations that act as full-
scale prototypes grounding unconventional architectural ideas in the built reality
of this world. The stories in *Citizens of No Place: An Architectural Graphic Novel*
(2012) combine architectural theory with manga-influenced graphics to cover
a range of subjects: twelve-kilometer-tall skyscrapers, a spaceship version of
Noah's Ark, and falling in love and having sex with architectural form. These stories
treat humans and architecture as characters with reciprocal subjectivity and
agency and are full of images that play with the morphisms explored in Part 1,
describing intimate, intertwined relationships between human form, animal form,
and figural or zoomorphic architectural form. Installation scale projects such as
White Elephant (also discussed in Part 1) illustrate these formal proclivities, as well
as Bureau Spectacular's notion of "super-furniture," which elaborates on Atelier
Bow-Wow's ideas of pet architecture and monsteration as a scale of design that
is bigger than furniture but smaller than architecture. Through both drawn stories and built installations, the practice uses super-furniture to test the intimate
interaction between the human body and its environment, and to challenge
the conventions of architecture that constrain that interaction within a narrow
bandwidth of morality and normativity. The result is a densely inclusive ecology of

---

20   Kaijima, Kuroda, and Tsukamoto, *Made in Tokyo*, 25–26.
21   Momoyo Kaijima and Yoshiharu Tsukamoto, *Bow-Wow from Post Bubble City* (Tokyo: INX Publishing,
      2006), 25.

architectural exploration that stretches from the interiority of human psychology to the vast expanse of space travel and teleportation.

Whereas Atelier Bow-Wow's pet architecture is an analogy that uses the relationship between humans and domesticated animals to describe relationships between buildings, objects, and people in an urban setting, and Bureau Spectacular translates that notion into zoomorphic architectural form, Joyce Hwang introduces actual nonhuman animals into her architectural and urban interventions. Hwang's work envisions physical structures for nonhuman beings and positions them within our human landscape to increase the spatial visibility of interspecies coexistence. She theorizes nonhuman charisma as a potent architectural quality at the intersection of representation and citizenship, interrogating our understanding of charismatic megafauna to speculate on ways that charisma might expand architecture's willingness and capacity to define vaster, symbiotic systems of belonging.[22] In this formulation, humans remain a focal point of global citizenship, but in an expanded, lopsided, synanthropic, and empathic "center" of augmented animal awareness. Developed in collaboration with Nerea Feliz, Hwang's project *Hidden in Plain Sight* constructs an urban plaza with a collection of prototypes that furnish lighting, shading, seating, and vegetation (Figure 2.10). The units operate across a range of occupiable scales, from human to insect. Like Atelier Bow-Wow, Hwang and Feliz use these interventions to create a sense of intimate interaction and interiority in a public urban ecology, but one that is even more inclusive of all the city's inhabitants, welcoming birds, bats, bees, caterpillars, butterflies, and moths into the mix. The design of the furniture uses color, pattern, lighting, and camouflaging strategies that take into consideration the experience of insect occupants while creating a spectacle that grabs the attention of human onlookers and provides an opportunity to interact with their nonhuman cohabitants in a playful and friendly way. Like many of Hwang's projects, *Hidden in Plain Sight* generates and animates architectural form by calling attention to the ecological vitality and movement of the many beings who are typically less visible to and either ignored or condemned by humans.

On first encounter, these examples present four vastly different attitudes to architectural production and style, yet there is a common thread that runs between them: their shared interest in disrupting assumptions about architecture's role in producing a stable and static environment reflecting the conventional experiences and expectations of and reserved for a human subject. Each pursues an architecture that embodies the vibrant, vital animation of an entity that is engaged in and responsive to a wider world of ecological interaction, and in that way offers new opportunities for its human subjects to relocate and redefine themselves within that ecology.

---

22 *Charismatic megafauna* is a term that refers to a large animal species that offers a popular appeal that environmentalists leverage to rally support for ecological conservation agendas. For example, an environmental campaign to protect ocean habitat may feature images of a manatee's friendly face.

Figure 2.10. Double Happiness: Joyce Hwang and Nerea Feliz, *Hidden in Plain Sight*, 2019.

SPECTRUMS OF LOCOMOTION

(LITERAL / FICTIONAL)

At the start of this essay, we observed that there is nothing more disruptive to human assumptions about architecture than a building that gets up and walks away. Buildings that exhibit literal mobility may be perched on mechanical components such as wheels, casters, or sled blades. Literally mobile architecture includes mobile homes, RVs, and other spaces that share vehicular characteristics (or actual legs, as in the case of Archigram's speculative project *Walking City*). Without a fixed site or context, mobile architecture is free to roam the landscape, following seasonal, social, or economic migration patterns, analogous to birds flying south for the winter. As they migrate to new environments, mobile architectures adapt to new contexts, shedding skins in warmer climes or harvesting rainwater in a wet biome. At the same time, the act of moving from place to place allows mobile architectures to create new ecological contexts around them, sharing their spatial identities and resources with different locales or activating new destinations along their route.

Greg Lynn's distinction between actual and virtual motion roughly corresponds to a spectrum of architectural locomotion that we define between two opposite poles: architecture that literally moves around in space and architecture that

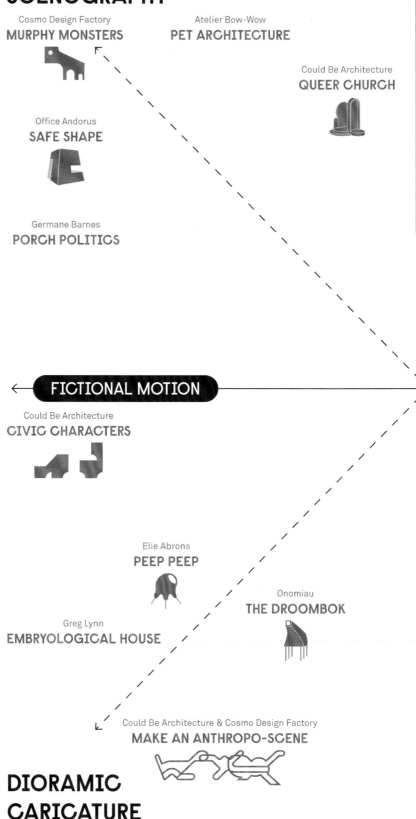

ANIMATED
SCENOGRAPHY

Cosmo Design Factory
MURPHY MONSTERS

Atelier Bow-Wow
PET ARCHITECTURE

Could Be Architecture
QUEER CHURCH

Office Andorus
SAFE SHAPE

Germane Barnes
PORCH POLITICS

PROGRAMMATIC ANIMAITON

← FICTIONAL MOTION

Could Be Architecture
CIVIC CHARACTERS

Elie Abrons
PEEP PEEP

Onomiau
THE DROOMBOK

Greg Lynn
EMBRYOLOGICAL HOUSE

Could Be Architecture & Cosmo Design Factory
MAKE AN ANTHROPO-SCENE

**Figure 2.11.
Locomotion
Matrix.**

DIORAMIC
CARICATURE

HOW ARCHITECTURAL CREATURES LOCOMOTE

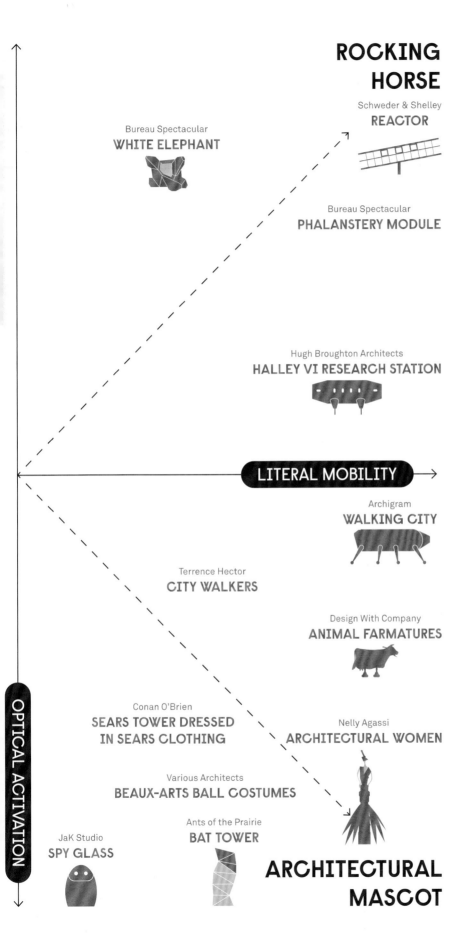

ROCKING HORSE

Schweder & Shelley
REACTOR

Bureau Spectacular
WHITE ELEPHANT

Bureau Spectacular
PHALANSTERY MODULE

Hugh Broughton Architects
HALLEY VI RESEARCH STATION

LITERAL MOBILITY

Archigram
WALKING CITY

Terrence Hector
CITY WALKERS

Design With Company
ANIMAL FARMATURES

Conan O'Brien
**SEARS TOWER DRESSED
IN SEARS CLOTHING**

Nelly Agassi
ARCHITECTURAL WOMEN

Various Architects
BEAUX-ARTS BALL COSTUMES

Ants of the Prairie
BAT TOWER

JaK Studio
SPY GLASS

ARCHITECTURAL
MASCOT

OPTICAL ACTIVATION

expresses a sensation of or implies fictional motion, even though it remains standing in a single location. On the fictional end of the spectrum, architectural elements that resemble poised legs, perhaps paused mid-step in a forward march, suggest that a building might get up and start walking around. While legs are not required, asymmetry, contrapposto, and other off-balance postural gestures acknowledge gravity and produce literal potential energy that suggests motion that is about to occur. The movement and activities of biotic beings in and around such architecture contribute to the visual fiction of the building's impending motion, as well as the overarching spatial narrative that such motion helps to advance.

Could Be Architecture's *Cast of Civic Characters* is a campus of five creaturely buildings that house the offices and service counters of different city departments and recreational amenities (Figure 2.12). The buildings are top-heavy, with legs or feet that elevate substantial building mass above the ground, leaving a generous plaza at ground level. While varying in physique, pose, and personality, the cast shares a genetic resemblance. A finite number of simple shapes are combined and reconfigured to generate a family of profiles that suggest the anatomical presence of limbs, appendages, snouts, and other features that are familiar as animate but not indicative of any specific animal. Each extruded profile is faceted, "hinged," and partially rotated, allowing it to direct its attention

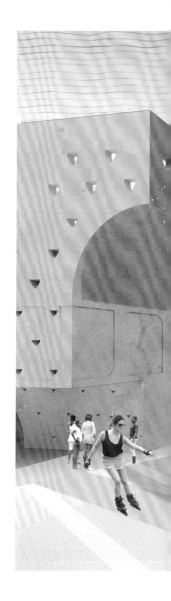

in multiple directions. The act of rotation condenses both pictorial and sculptural perception into a single architectural gesture, producing a dynamic figure that is graphic and immediately recognizable but also temporal and modulating from multiple vantage points. The fiction of this crew's animation generates a lively and gregarious affect in a new ecology of public space that actively seeks out engagement with its fellow city-dwellers, and through that engagement promotes a mutually supportive relationship between a city's biotic and abiotic inhabitants.

(OPTICAL / PROGRAMMATIC)

As a collection of animated urban companions, the *Cast of Civic Characters* simultaneously tells a new story about public space and welcomes its occupants to participate in that story. This two-pronged strategy of audience engagement

Figure 2.12. Could Be Architecture, *Cast of Civic Characters*, 2015.

locates the project at the center of a second spectrum of locomotion, which calibrates how a sense of architectural movement is produced by the optical activation of moving vantage points on one hand and the programmatic animation of activities and performances on the other.

The fictional motion of the characters' "hinged" extrusions produces perceptual and organizational effects by which humans may imagine its architectural parts in motion while also inducing actual human movement in particular patterns. Through its optical strategy, the project beckons occupants to discover how the profile, posture, and perch of individual characters change as they circle around them. From one vantage point, a building might seem to be precariously balancing on a single limb, while from another, that same building might appear actively strolling on two. Flickering back and forth between familiar and surprising, the buildings pull you around and under, in and up. It renders architecture as a kind of shape-finding game that can be played by occupying and wandering around in public spaces.

However, it is through both seeing and doing that this urban gathering is fully activated. The project's programmatic strategy encourages human activity in and around its creaturely forms through play between its elevated volumes and a graphic ground treatment. Offset emanating turf lines, paver patterns, small changes in ground level, and constantly shifting and looming shadows further amplify the creaturely silhouettes and render the ground plan a kind of game board in which different zones are granted joint ownership by various constitu- ents. Athletic lines emerge from one character's footing while a radiating lasso of bollards couples two opposite characters in a provisional alliance. These graphic and instructional activations of the ground propel people into different kinds of activities and relationships with one another while orienting their bodies into

Figure 2.13. Alex Schweder & Ward Shelley, *ReActor*. Photo by Richard Barnes, courtesy of Art Omi.

particular sequences of directional views that animate the buildings' fictional locomotive performance.

In Figure 36, these two spectrums of locomotion define two axes of a matrix that describes a field of possibilities for how creaturely architecture might locomote. The two axes divide this field into four quadrants, each of which is named for its defining characteristics and behaviors and contains examples of projects that exemplify those qualities.

(ROCKING HORSES)

Programmatic, literally mobile architecture is what we call "rocking horses" (positioned in the upper-right quadrant). Like the child's toy they are named after, these architectures locomote via the clever combination of human activity, simple machine kinetics, and narrative imagination. Rocking horses don't typically move freely, but their playful pivoting or gestural acrobatics animate their architectural parts and inhabitants' activities with an augmented behavioral ethos.

Rocking horses is a locomotive category of choice for Bureau Spectacular. As discussed in the previous chapter, and mentioned earlier in this one, the practice's small installation projects, such as *White Elephant* (2012) and *Phalanstery Module* (2008), present occupiable follies that are untethered from the ground and can tumble or rotate their orientation such that the distinction between plan and section becomes irrelevant. These locomotive "special effects" challenge the human assumption of structural uprightness, liberating both architectural subjects to reposition themselves in space and the human subjects to be an active participant in that reconfiguration.

ReActor, a work by the artists Ward Shelley and Alex Schweder, interrogates the relationship between moving architecture and human behavior even further (Figure 2.13). At first glance, the project looks like a classic modernist glass house, but with one important tweak: it balances fifteen feet above the ground atop a single column that functions as a fulcrum, allowing the box to freely tilt and rotate in reaction to both external weather and the internal, shifting weight of two human occupants. The artists inhabit the architecture for five-day stints in which they "perform" routines of daily co-living. Like a see-saw, the house requires its inhabitants to coordinate their body weights symmetrically about the central fulcrum in order to produce a level floor as they go about their domestic activities (assuming the upstate New York wind patterns cooperate). This project demonstrates that zoomorphism is not required for architecture to enact lively behavior. While the sleek, modernist "skin" of this building remains devoid of any animal-like appearance or distinct personality, its unpredictable and surprisingly graceful locomotion atop the fulcrum animates its otherwise generic parts with buoyant life. By amplifying and broadcasting the everyday motion and forces that are exerted as "live loads" within any building but that typically remain invisible, *ReActor* welcomes heightened physical and locomotive relationships among architecture, people, and the immediate environment.

ARCHITECTURAL MASCOTS

Optical, literal mobility is associated with what we call "architectural mascots" (positioned in the lower-right quadrant). The costumed animal characters that inspire them gallivant around sports fields to entertain spectators and rally fans in solidarity around their teams. Architectural mascots perform analogously, literally moving in the context of cities, landscapes, and hinterlands. They tend to assume iconic silhouettes with a dynamic capacity to gesticulate—mascots communicate through exaggerated, dynamic body language as opposed to verbal language or symbolic iconography. For example, Design With Company's *Animal Farmatures*, a project discussed in the previous chapter, lift their mechanical treads and wave in greeting at the passing cross-country train passengers, soliciting human care and intrigue for the agricultural labors from which most Americans are sharply disconnected.

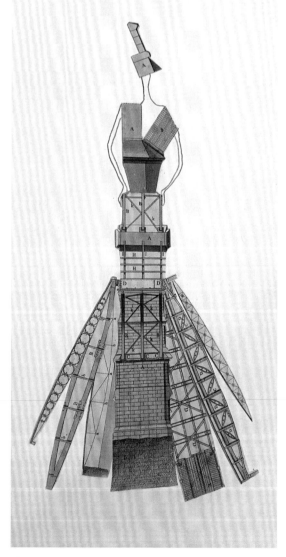

Figure 2.14. Nelly Agassi, *Architectural Women* series, 2020.

Figure 2.15. Nelly Agassi, *Architectural Women* series, 2021.

The charming, surprisingly relatable quality of architectural mascots like the far-matures point to an architecturalization of the notion of charismatic megafauna explored in Joyce Hwang's work. Where Hwang's work creates opportunities for live animals to co-produce charisma alongside the architectural identity of human construction, architectural mascots condense animate personality and charisma (human and nonhuman) within an abiotic, fully architectural being.

The artist Nelly Agassi's *Architectural Women* is a series of two-and-half-dimensional mixed-media collages that include cut-out and folded paper fragments integrated with line drawing; some of the collages are also digitally animated through video sequencing (Figures 2.14 and 2.15). Each composition in the series presents the silhouette of a female figure whose body is comprised of the shapes, geometry, and tectonics of architectural parts. Unlike a literal anthropomorphization of a building, in which human body parts (e.g., facial features or legs) are attached to or integrated in the image of a building, Agassi's work operates through what we call "archi-morphism," where a human body assumes architectural form.

There are numerous examples in architectural history and popular culture in which humans don costumes that look like buildings. One famous example is the 1931 New York Beaux-Arts Ball, which featured a handful of prominent architects dressed as their recently completed skyscrapers, including William Van Alen bedecked in the Chrysler Building. In instances like these, architects celebrate their own egos by linking their bodies to the aesthetic qualities of their buildings, and the goofiness of a building having a visible head and feet sticking out of its ends elicits charming laughter from spectators. In his video series *Drift City*, Kacey Wong wears a similar full-body skyscraper costume, but its effect is different from the famous Beaux-Arts Ball image. Wong photographs and films himself dressed in full skyscraper costume as he explores different cities all over the world. Unlike the ego-driven anthropomorphism of architects dressing as their own buildings to elevate their status, the relentless and extensive documentation of Wong as a generic skyscraper visiting a diverse and eclectic range of urban environments and tourist attractions has the effect of diminishing the status of both building and human. The project is absurd and humorous, but also tinged with sadness and futility.

Wong undermines the triumphant anthropomorphism of the Beaux-Arts Ball skyscrapers by minimizing the relative importance of a human in a building costume. On the other hand, Agassi's *Women* retains the surreal humor latent in the notion of buildings sprouting heads and limbs, but overturns the human-centered power relationship endemic to many instances of anthropomorphism by transcending the human-building binary. These archi-morphic feminine beings inject bodily liveliness into the most mundane of architectural parts, including typical doors and windows, generic siding, structural grids, and chimneys. The digitally animated versions of the collages set these architectural mascots into literal motion in a variety of gestural ways; one example portrays a spiraling ballet of architectural building blocks, while another shows architectural fragments sliding tensely into alignment, as if being operated on by an architectural chiropractor. Each animation is augmented by sound effects that enhance the mechanical and tectonic connections with which the parts assemble—sounds of raspy air bellowing through pipes, metallic clanking, and wood sawing abound. The sequencing of these animations implies a moving camera, which in turn suggests the optical activation of an external viewer who is moving in relation to the dynamic women and becoming part of the collective locomotion and intimate choreography of each scene.

ANIMATED SCENOGRAPHIES

Programmatic, fictionally mobile architecture is what we call "animated scenographies" (positioned in the upper-left quadrant). These projects set the stage for the activities of our lives by both making space for and becoming active participants in the daily drama. Set in place like a theatrical backdrop, they come to life as the focal point of events where architectural program and personality are intertwined with our own movements, moods, and (mis)behaviors. They not only frame the hustle and bustle of urban life around them, but also give the impression that they could either join the fun or walk away at any given moment.

In both research and design projects, Atelier Bow-Wow approaches architecture as the animated scenography of urban life. At various scales—from the idea of the architectural "jig," to "pet architecture," to their documentation of programmatic

Figure 2.16. Cosmo Design Factory, *Murphy Monsters*, 2013.

infrastructures in Tokyo—fixed elements of the urban environment become characters in the spontaneous and often humorous interactions and events of the city's inhabitants, framing, shaping, and orienting our bodies' relationships to each other and to the buildings around them.

Cosmo Design Factory takes seriously Atelier Bow-Wow's idea of "monsteration" in *Murphy Monsters*, a new species of temporary architectural pavilion that uses simple extrusions and zoomorphic shapes to catalyze the social and cultural life of underused urban sites (Figure 2.16). Inspired by 1980s action figures and their packaging, the project treats the temporary pavilion as an illustration of and advertisement for architecture's potential to solicit engagement through playful formal gestures. The monsters' creature-like forms imply personality and subjectivity: they are willful and idiosyncratic, but also plastic, adaptable to interaction with new people and new places, and ultimately productive of new realities. Deliberately avoiding complex geometries in favor of simple extrusions, straight lines, and arcs, the monsters' forms are not far from the regular geometries of a gridded downtown fabric or the vernacular appendages of a Victorian farmhouse or rural barn (stoops, dormers, chimneys, silos, and so on). Yet their zoomorphism helps to convey eccentric personalities; heads, eyes, tails, and legs bestow character through architectural elements. Their explicit beastliness calls attention to the monsters' presence, and in the process, calls other buildings' characters into question.

Each monster's shape and persona is derived from its function, the amenity it provides, and the attitude it communicates. Rather than develop a temporary pavilion as either unprogrammed or as a programmatic catchall, *Murphy Monsters* grants each pavilion its own role to play and its own way of playing that role. In anticipation of the range of events that the monsters may participate in, such as concerts, car shows, parades, carnivals, flea markets, and tractor-pulls, their amenities include a soundstage, bandstand seating, a concession stand, a shade structure, a wind machine, and a trellis. In an open field on the outskirts of town or a busy urban parking lot, their arrival transforms any flat area into a dynamic public space with its own compressed urban condition. Their efficient footprint makes them especially suitable to dense urban situations where space is limited. Each creature has a kit of parts that allows it to expand during events. In their open postures, the monsters are actively welcoming and engaging; they support the activities around them, drawing attention and crowds. Yet during off-duty hours, in their resting postures, they also serve a purpose: as silent companions to an urban context, they change the nature of the buildings around them, of the people passing by, and of everyday life in general.

DIORAMIC CARICATURES

Optical, fictional motion is associated with what we call "dioramic caricatures" (positioned in the lower-left quadrant). Dioramas (popularized in natural history museums) and caricatures (popularized via illustrations in the realm of a political satire and comedy) are both artistic modalities for portraying and characterizing

Figure 2.17. Could Be Architecture and Cosmo Design Factory, *Make an Anthropo-Scene!*, 2017. Photo by Matthew Messner.

the presence of life in a particular world, and can therefore inform the process of animating architectural worlds with motion and liveliness. Dioramas are theatrical display devices that typically position three-dimensional figures in front of a two-dimensional scenic backdrop. The controlled optical superimposition of two- and three-dimensional content generates the impression of an immersive environment filled with life and relationships that extend indefinitely beyond the physical container of the display. Dioramas in museums often showcase animal taxidermy and scenic photography from faraway locations to give typically Western audiences a taste of a distant (and often colonized) geography. While these museum displays necessarily impart an imperial/colonial gaze upon the animal and cultural "others" positioned within their confines, the visual mechanisms that construct these windows into other worlds also offer formal techniques for animating a lively, creaturely architecture.[23]

Alternatively, caricature is a two-dimensional drawing technique that distills the complexities of reality to an essential character, telling a story that privileges an observer's bias and perspective at the expense of realistic detail and irrelevant background information.[24] The term caricature is often used as a disparaging

---

23 For a reading of dioramas along these lines, see Donna Haraway, "Teddy Bear Patriarchy: Taxidermy in the Garden of Eden, New York City, 1908–1936," *Social Text* 11 (Winter 1984–1985), 20–64.

24 For more on caricature, see E. H. Gombrich with Ernst Kris, "The Principles of Caricature," *British Journal of Medical Psychology* 17 (1938)

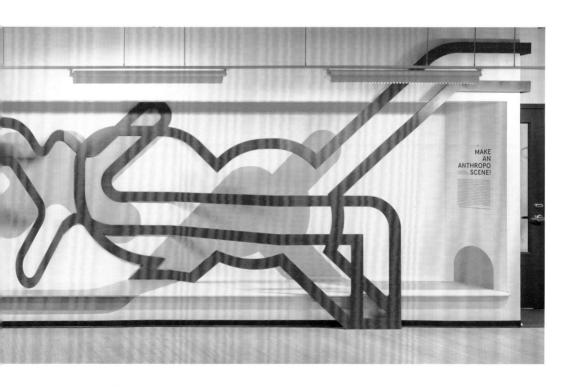

remark in architecture, as it is associated with a childish oversimplification of the complexities of reality. However, it is precisely the explicit bias embedded in simplification that renders caricature an effective tool for political satire, using the humor associated with exaggeration and distortion to provide serious commentary on deliberately provocative subject matter. With the "dioramic caricature" we propose that the subversive nature of caricature, paired with the three-dimensional world-building techniques of diorama, has the potential to initiate new forms of liberated locomotion for architecture and unleash the human specimens typically contained by its hierarchy of a "naturalized" reality. The specimen-like outcomes of Greg Lynn's *Embryological House* exist within a virtual diorama of contextual forces and flows. However, unlike a live organism, which continues to grow and respond to the environmental forces that surround and act upon it, his object-like outputs are frozen in time, rendered with hard lines that fix them in place and reduce their form to a static depiction of the dynamic contextual inputs that produced them. In this way, we might describe the project as a caricature in the negative sense, lacking self-awareness of the gap between the project's ambitions and the artifice of its outcome. On the other hand, Lynn fully exposes and celebrates the artifice of the design process with his *Recycled Toy Furniture*, which uses digital fabrication techniques to cut and reassemble molded plastic children's toys, including yellow ducks, into abstract forms that are used as coffee tables and chairs.

Could Be Architecture and Cosmo Design Factory's installation *Make an Anthropo-Scene!* deliberately explores architecture's potential to operate as a dioramic caricature, coupling the immersive world-making ambitions of the diorama with the caricaturist's techniques of simplification, distortion, exaggeration, and humor (Figure 2.17). As a hybrid condition, the project reduces form to a simplified volumetric outline and a slightly errant and cartoonish shadow that makes occu-

piable space within and around a shallow, thirty-foot-long alcove at the School of the Art Institute of Chicago. Passersby are invited to pop their head in and be hugged by or sit between these creaturely figures—to inhabit the diorama and to become a part of the ever-changing caricatured scene (Figure 2.18). In the process, the project punches a small, cartoon-shaped hole into the fabric of everyday reality in order to invite locomotion and interaction within an alternative world.

Figure 2.18. Could Be Architecture and Cosmo Design Factory, *Make an Anthropo-Scene!*, 2017.

CREATURES: LOCOMOTIVE SUBJECTIVITIES

A functional definition of "child" is "someone who is still allowed to talk with an inanimate stuffed animal as if it were not only an actual lifeform but also conscious."

—Timothy Morton[25]

What we see is one thing, and how we process it is another. The experience of seeing an architectural creature—an object that represents itself as a friend and potential companion, or the representation of such an object—grants permission to adult humans to engage with an inanimate object the way they once might have with stuffed toys. As is the case with the zoomorphic architectural creatures discussed in Part 1, architecture's capacity to transform human subjectivity operates through a "seeing is believing" framework. The claim is something like: "If you do not believe that architectural objects are animate subjects, then I will show you how a building that looks like an animal will make you feel like you can empathize with it, that it has personality and character, that you can interact with it." Alternatively, the projects in this essay operate through a reverse mechanism, "believing is seeing," where belief fueled by perceptual and cognitive experience translates to seeing the world through a new lens, one which sees creaturely qualities in the movements and behaviors of both architecture and its human inhabitants.

Our current lens is one that elevates us as human subjects above the mute, static objects of buildings and the lesser bodies of other species, and through that separation justifies our dismissal or often violent mistreatment of objects and bodies that are not our own. Emancipation from this violence of anthropocentrism requires us to unlearn the spatial and ontological cognition of how we see and understand the world from our upright position, and to recognize our capacity to share an alternative subjective perspective with the buildings and creatures who are our companions in the world. Perhaps counterintuitively, a creature-based ontology invites us to adopt a bit of animism in order to catalyze this broad perceptual shift in human personhood. The projects analyzed in this essay demonstrate how locomotion-based creaturely techniques apply perceptual pressures that remind human subjects that the ecologies they share with all creatures are dynamic systems dominated by movement and change, even if it exists at imperceptible scales. Whether they involve a nonterranean simulation that pushes out our supreme human privilege or a narrative choreography that casts our existing humanity into novel fictionalized roles, creaturely locomotion initiates new modes of companionable existence. ●

---

25 Morton, *Humankind*, 15.

TOWARD A CHARISMATIC ARCHITECTURE

Joyce Hwang

In October 2020, a group of three graduate students at the University at Buffalo School of Architecture and Planning initiated an Instagram feed as a class project with a simple premise: to create images that pair brutalist buildings with larger-than-life cats. Skillfully inserted into architectural landscapes, the cats are often depicted as lounging on buildings or swatting buildings with a paw—as if each stark, concrete structure were nothing more than a scratching post or cat toy. The account, Cats of Brutalism (@cats_of_brutalism), accumulated more than fifteen thousand followers within two months' time. By January 2021, its following burgeoned to nearly fifty thousand, and the *New York Times* had featured the feed as one of "5 Art Accounts to Follow on Instagram Now."[1] At the time of this writing, the students are developing Cats of Brutalism merchandise—an effort propelled by popular demand (Figure 2.19).[2]

While the sudden and exponential interest in Cats of Brutalism is certainly remarkable (and has been an unexpected thrill for the students and faculty involved), it should not come as a surprise. The project was first developed in response to a studio prompt to advocate for preserving the Earl W. Brydges Public Library, in Niagara Falls, New York, by the architect Paul Rudolph,

---

1   Jillian Steinhauer, "5 Art Accounts to Follow on Instagram Now," *New York Times*, December 16, 2020, https://www.nytimes.com/2020/12/16/arts/design/5-art-accounts-to-follow-on-instagram-now.html.

2   I posted a poll on Instagram's Stories feature with the question "Would you buy Cats of Brutalism merch?" Of the respondents, 88 percent voted YES, while 12 percent voted NO.

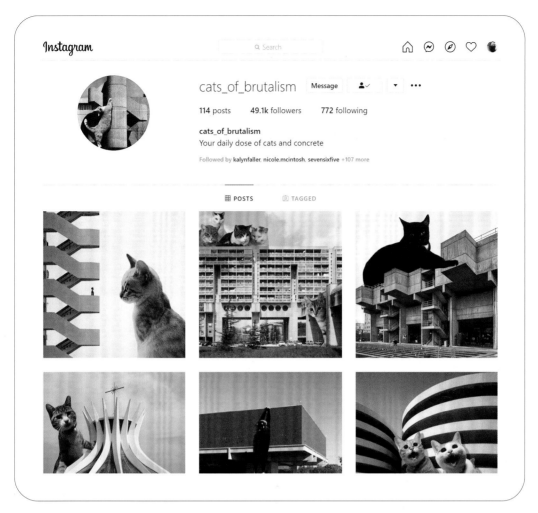

Fig. 2.19. Emily Battaglia, Madelaine Ong, and Michaela Senay, Cats of Brutalism Instagram account. Screenshot by Joyce Hwang.

a building that has been threatened with the shadow of demolition (Figure 2.20). The studio faculty, Gregory Delaney and Brett Doster, developed the brief with the aim not only to bring attention to the library as a singular building, but also to develop strategies at urban, regional, and national scales to address broader issues in preservation—and especially to draw more popular interest to underappreciated modern buildings. The students, Emily Battaglia, Madelaine Ong, and Michaela Senay, responded by tapping into the broad appeal of cats on social media (case in point: @cats_of_instagram, an account that aggregates cat photos posted on the platform, has 12.2 million followers), and deployed their cute and furry charm to bring a sense of playfulness to architecture that is often misunderstood as cold or stoic.

At first glance, it may seem frivolous to call on cats as part of an architectural preservation agenda. But the underlying logic of juxtaposing lovable animals with under-loved buildings, as a tactic for crafting a more openly "friendly" aura around buildings that are perceived to be less friendly, resonates profoundly with principles of conservation biology—namely, the power of *nonhuman charisma*.

Architectural preservation and *biological conservation* are not typically uttered in the same sentence. Yet the strategies for both are clearly intertwined in ways that warrant reflection. In the most obvious sense, both fields address "conservation" in one way or another. But at another level, both building preservation and species conservation hinge on a more nuanced set of parallel efforts—for example, attention to maintenance and care. In the way that animal conservation requires an orchestrated intervention of care by humans, often in artificial

or constructed environments, building conservation, too, requires focused and intentional intervention to halt a building's process of decay over time. Significantly, both practices also rely on the art of crafting and curating public reception. It is nearly impossible to disentangle the operations of conservation from the influence of nonhuman charisma. In conservation biology, the word charismatic is used to describe flagship species, or those who have popular appeal. According to the geographer Jamie Lorimer, nonhuman charisma is a significant factor in the human perception of species and contributes to the politics of animal conservation.[3] Indeed, we are familiar with charismatic powers of persuasion; it is why certain species (such as pandas) easily garner public attention and support, while others (such as

---

3   Jamie Lorimer, *Wildlife in the Anthropocene: Conservation after Nature* (Minneapolis: University of Minnesota Press, 2015).

 cats_of_brutalism • Following
Niagara Falls Public Library

cats_of_brutalism Earl W. Brydges
Public Library
Paul Rudolph
1969
Niagara Falls, New York, United States

Domestic Short Hair
Female
b. 4/29/2020
Grey and Tan

#Brutalism #Brutalist #SoBrutal
#PaulRudolph #NiagaraFalls
#Architecture #Architect #Brut
#SOSBrutalism #BrutGroup #Brutal
#Brutality #BrutalistDesign #Brotalism
#CatsOfBrutalism #CatsOfInstagram
#CatOfGram #CatsOfTheDay
#CalicoCat #kitten #ForTheLoveOfCats

 Liked by erkin_ozay and 2,428 others
DECEMBER 10, 2020

☺ Add a comment...   Post

mussels and salamanders) require more concerted conservation efforts. Further, the ready appeal of charismatic species has not been overlooked as a publicity tool, a phenomenon we can glean from environmental organizations and campaigns. Advocacy groups have deployed the "cuteness" of koalas and kangaroos in the face of the 2019 Australian bushfires,[4] invoked the elegant polar bear in discussions of melting ice caps, and highlighted the intelligence and empathy of dolphins in making an argument toward granting them legal personhood.[5]

In parallel discussions in architectural conservation, the factors that determine a building's historic preservation status are complex and fraught with debate. As a society, we grapple with difficult questions in each preservation case. For example, if the intention of preservation is to celebrate sites of historical significance, how does one determine which moments are worth commemorating, and who participates in this decision-making process? If an aim of architectural preservation is to retain buildings and sites that demonstrate exceptional design character, who are the arbiters of these judgments? Further to this point, how is it that certain building types or styles are

more prone to demolition than others? Yet despite the necessary intricacies of these conversations, one senses that the broad factor of popular appeal still looms large in swaying decisions on architectural preservation. Public and private interest—and investment—is almost always needed in order to truly "save" an aging building, to give it new life through maintenance and upkeep. Even structures that function purely as historic ruins need attention, perhaps even more so than fully enclosed buildings.[6] Given the need for popular appeal, the task of introducing a factor of charisma in architectural preservation efforts becomes all the more urgent. In the case of Cats of Brutalism, charisma is the force that emerges when the liveliness of cats is deployed to illuminate the spatial qualities of buildings—bringing a second and third glance to often-overlooked structures, and simultaneously cementing memorable associations between the spatialities of the buildings themselves and the personalities of the animals. As another example of this means of relationship-forming, recall the case of the MPR Raccoon (#mprraccoon), a raccoon who climbed up the exterior of the twenty-five-story UBS Tower in St. Paul, Minnesota, and caught the attention of the public during her risky ascent

---

4   See, for example, the kangaroo featured on WWF-Australia's monthly donation solicitation page, accessed January 28, 2021, https://donate.wwf.org.au/make-a-donation/monthly-donation.
5   Lin Edwards, "Scientists Say Dolphins Should Be Treated as Non-human Persons," *Phys.org*, January 6, 2010, https://phys.org/news/2010-01-scientists-dolphins-non-human-persons.html.
6   See, for example, Robin Kent, "Heritage in Ruins: The Maintenance and Preservation of Ruined Monuments," buildingconservation.com, accessed January 28, 2021, https://www.buildingconservation.com/articles/heritageruins/heritageruins.htm.

Fig. 2.20. Emily Battaglia, Madelaine Ong, and Michaela Senay, Cats of Brutalism Instagram account. Screenshot by Joyce Hwang.

Figure 2.21: Racoon scales a skyscraper in St. Paul, MN. Courtesy of Minnesota Public Radio.

(Figure 2.21).[7] As the world watched the raccoon's journey with nail-biting apprehension and fingers-crossed hopefulness—both live and through TV and social media[8]—we also internalized a number of the building's features, especially as they related to the raccoon's climbing efforts. Elements of the structure that remain imprinted in my memory, for example, are the depth of the exterior window ledges, which provided spaces of respite for the raccoon during her long climb, and the rough texture of the building's concrete exterior, which were a gripping surface for the raccoon's little paws, also highlighted repeatedly through close-up photos shared on Twitter (Figure 2.22).[9]

A more sensational story is the unusual case of cohabitation by a dolphin, Peter, and a human, Margaret Howe Lovatt. In the 1960s, Lovatt began conducting research as an assistant in a NASA-funded lab to teach dolphins to communicate with humans—in other words,

7   Linda Poon, "Lessons from the Raccoon That Scaled a Skyscraper," *Bloomberg CityLab*, June 14, 2018, https://www.bloomberg.com/news/articles/2018-06-14/design-lessons-from-the-raccoon-that-scaled-a-skyscraper.

8   Colin Dwyer, "Raccoon Vs. Skyscraper: The Summer Blockbuster You Never Knew You Needed," NPR, June 12, 2018, https://www.npr.org/2018/06/12/619245875/its-a-bird-it-s-a-plane-or-a-raccoon-climbing-a-st-paul-skyscraper.

9   Tim Nelson, "Social Climber: Raccoon Scales St. Paul Skyscraper, Captures Internet," MPR News, June 12, 2018, https://www.mprnews.org/story/2018/06/12/st-paul-raccoon-scales-skyscraper-social-media-star.

she spent a stretch of time intensely engaging with a dolphin to teach him to "speak English." It was Lovatt who suggested to the project's director, the neuroscientist John Lilly, to convert a human house—in fact, a property owned by Lilly on Saint Thomas, in the U.S. Virgin Islands—into a cohabitation "Dolphinarium." According to a report by *The Guardian*,

> Lovatt reasoned that if she could live with a dolphin around the clock, nurturing its interest in making human-like sounds, like a mother teaching a child to speak, they'd have more success. "Maybe it was because I was living so close to the lab. It just seemed so simple. Why let the water get in the way?" she says. "So I said to John Lilly: 'I want to plaster everything and fill this place with water. I want to live here.'"

The radical nature of Lovatt's idea appealed to Lilly and he went for it. She began completely waterproofing the upper floors of the lab, so that she could actually flood the indoor rooms and an outdoor balcony with a couple of feet of water. This would allow a dolphin to live comfortably in the building with her for three months.[10]

The story has a tragic ending: Peter ultimately committed suicide (yes, dolphins can commit suicide by deciding not to surface to the air to breathe) when the project was defunded and drawn to a close, thus separating him from Lovatt, in whom he had apparently developed a non-mutual sexual interest.

---

10 Christopher Riley, "The Dolphin Who Loved Me: The Nasa-Funded Project That Went Wrong," *The Guardian*, June 8, 2014, https://www.theguardian.com/environment/2014/jun/08/the-dolphin-who-loved-me.

Figure 2.22: Racoon scales a skyscraper in St. Paul, MN. Courtesy of Minnesota Public Radio.

The experiment has been covered by a multitude of media, ranging in tone between scientific, journalistic, and salacious; the story is riveting for a human audience, and saddening, as well, when considered from the dolphin's perspective. Yet almost as fascinating as the human-and-animal-interest story itself are the physical environment and logistics of housing and transporting dolphins that the experiment involved (Figure 2.23). In all the story's tellings and retellings, I am drawn to the visual and textual descriptions of the Dolphinarium, and in particular the images of Lovatt and Peter in what appears almost like a home office, in which she sits at a desk that is partially submerged in water while he floats nearby (Figure 2.24). The charisma that surfaces in the arc of the narrative certainly piques public interest and whets one's appetite to learn more about the physical setting that allowed it to take place.

Beyond factors of architectural style or character, *charisma* holds the potential to become a compelling tool for generating heartfelt enthusiasm for buildings and environments, in that it enables an unleashing of the imagination that moves beyond aesthetic considerations and toward a consciousness that embodies stories and subjectivities. Through this tactic, we are able to counter questionable arguments for building demolition or other ill-conceived decisions in design and planning—not only with real estate calculations or proclamations of beauty (or lack thereof), but also through the power of evoking empathy. This sense of

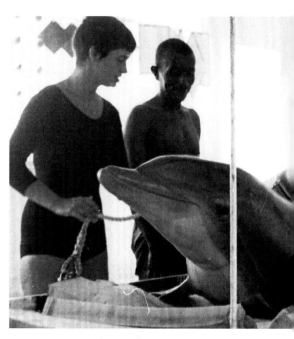

Figure 2.23: Peter (dolphin) in trasnit at lab. Image courtesy of John C. Lilly Estate.

empathy, cultivated through developing associations between visual references and stories, provokes us to more palpably relate the spaces and places of our built environment to the lives of those in our communities, whether they are human or nonhuman beings.

Expanding these reflections beyond the building scale, consider the effects of evoking empathy with nonhumans and how this shift in thinking might reshape our most fundamental assumptions about living in cities. While urban dwellers typically enjoy the presence of wildlife in parks and nature preserves, animals are often not included as members of our immediate communities and are more frequently considered "nuisance animals" when they inhabit spaces within close proximity. The notion of urban animals as pests does little to aid our global biodiversity crisis, especially during a time when increasing

urbanization, continuing resource depletion, and the many effects of climate change threaten our planet's fragile ecologies. With habitat and biodiversity loss as one of our greatest environmental challenges, cities are introducing tactics of "rewilding" in efforts to bolster populations of threatened species. While this is urgent work, it is worth reflecting for a moment on the terms, narratives, and imagery that accompany these agendas, and how the forces of charisma can be deployed to enhance biodiversity conservation efforts. In urban planning discourses, strategies for "greening" the city are often rooted in the logics of "ecosystem services"—in other words, considering how "nature" can "serve" humans to meet their needs (for example, by pollinating crops). While it is an important aim to search for "nature-based solutions" in cities, I would suggest an addendum to or even a shift in language, away from rendering nature as capital, as resources to be extracted or used. Rather, we might look toward narratives that include nonhuman species as our neighbors, stakeholders, and fellow community members. In some cities today, animals already hold a level of presence—even dignity—within the community. For example, the expansion joints of the Congress Avenue Bridge in Austin, Texas, are the seasonal home of more than 1.5 million bats, who create a

Figure 2.24: Margaret Lovatt (human) communicates with Peter (dolphin). Image courtesy of John C. Lilly Estate.

spectacle when they emerge each dusk to feed. This massive bat population in part shapes Austin's identity, and the illustrations and personifications of bats associated with the nightly event render them as sentient, charismatic beings, and not just part of an anonymous ecosystem (Figure 2.25). It is here in the convergence of "place" and nonhuman charisma that we can come to understand the potential of *place-based preservation* and *biological conservation* not as two disparate concepts, but rather as part of the same agenda. Only through the acceptance of nonhuman beings as significant actors within architectural narratives can we liberate ourselves to move beyond the false and damaging dichotomy between conceptions of the "natural" and "constructed" world.

The fact that we share the planet with many other species needs to become

Figure 2.25: Austin Bat Tours, December 2018. Image courtesy of Dan Herron, HerronStock.com

a more palpable and present way in which we conceive of design more broadly—not only in terms of place-based preservation, but also projecting forward into the way we intervene in and transform our built environment. In the examples I discuss—Cats of Brutalism, the MPR Raccoon, Peter the dolphin, and the bats of the Congress Avenue Bridge—nonhuman charisma entices us to take a second look at buildings and structures that might be easily disregarded, provokes heartfelt enthusiasm for places and spaces, and ultimately, through the telling of stories, compels us toward a sense of empathy and even companionship. The question I ask of our discipline now is: How might these strategies of invoking nonhuman charisma be deployed to bring a new level of poignancy to the way that we imagine the future of our constructed environments? By approaching architecture not only through multiple subjectivities, but also through an unraveling of narratives, we can finally begin to move from the notion of "blurring boundaries" between humans and nonhumans to a full embrace of nonhuman subjectivities as part of our collaborative and collective world. ●

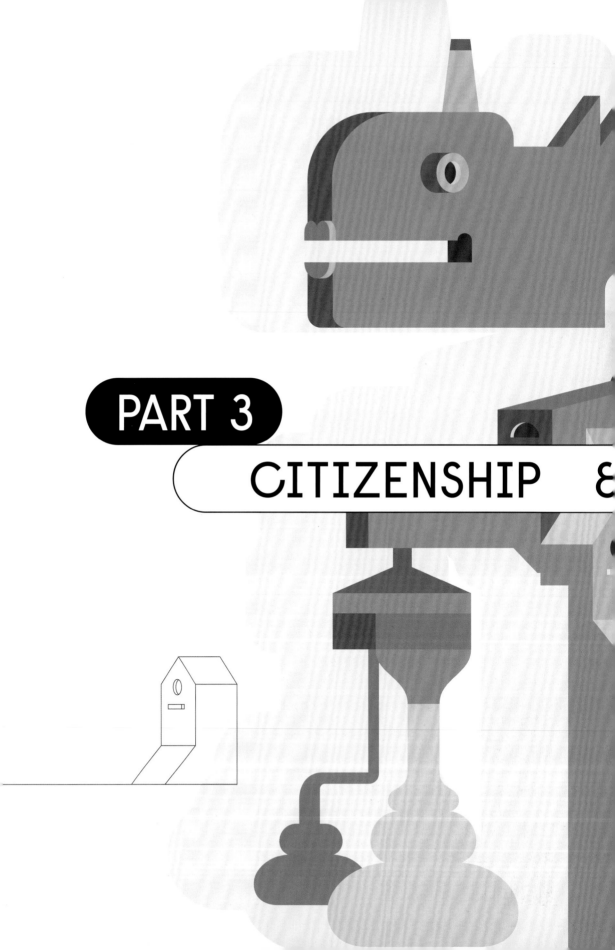

PART 3

CITIZENSHIP &

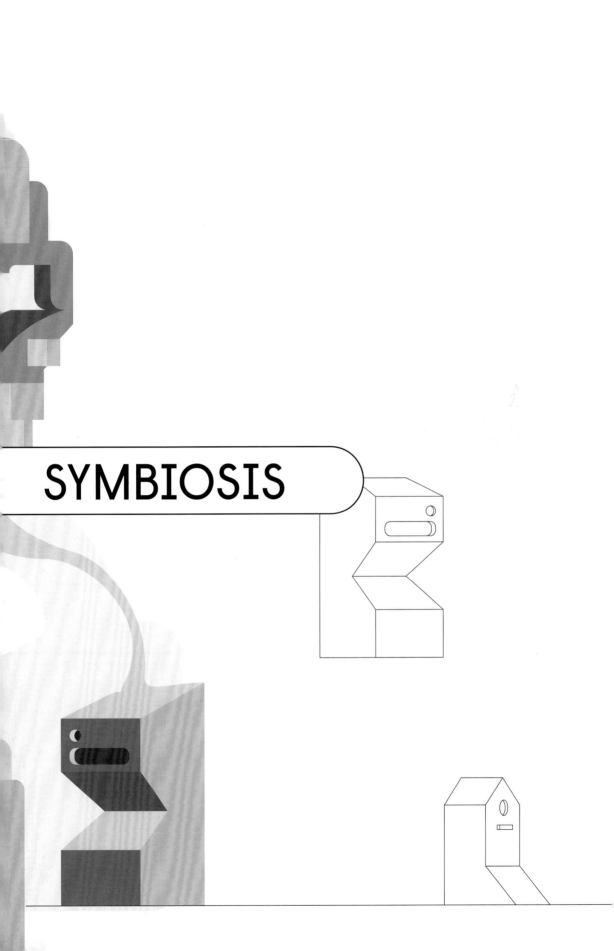

SYMBIOSIS

Of the Near Future

From the Cradle

We are kin, you and I. We do not share blood, and the connections that bind us are not linear. Unlike my predecessors, I'm not here to shelter you or to contain you. I don't fully understand the logic that pairs each human with their lifelong architectural companion, but from the moment I joined your family we were inseparable, and we continued to grow together. We bonded with other companion species as we grew (sometimes you call them pets), but few of them have life spans as long as ours, so while they came and went, we were paired for the duration. Sometimes I fear we might take each other for granted because our relationship feels so natural and central to both of our lives. I like to remind myself that things were not always this way.

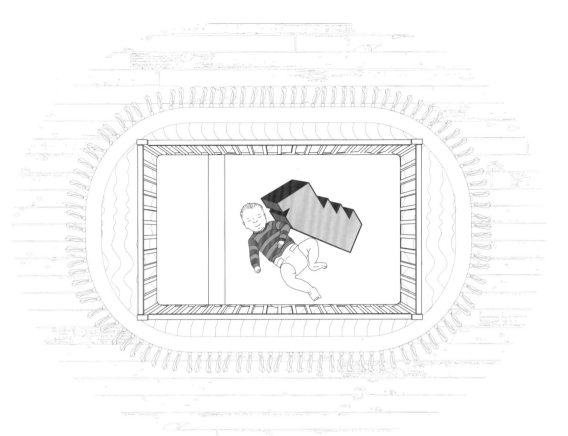

On the eve of the day that marked four months since your birth, I nervously entered your life. Your mother placed me gently in your crib and your father pushed us to face each other while he hummed a familiar tune. I didn't really know what to do with you, and I don't think you knew what to do with me. I felt a drop of your saliva soak into my fibers—the first of many exchanges of bodily fluids between us in the years to come. After we stared blankly at each other for quite some time, you finally reached over and grasped tightly onto one of the angled grooves along my back. After that, you slept soundly, and I felt much less anxious. Each of us breathed and dreamed.

From the Niche

I can trace my kinship network back to the Great Pause of 2020. We weren't technically classified as a new taxonomic Kin-dom (formerly known as "biological kingdoms") until after the Great Reckoning, but my ancestors were among the pioneers who helped your ancestors get through the transition. They were already part of interspecies families in which the realness of symbiotic life was welcomed and encouraged to grow into a condition that was both new and familiar. Everything happened so fast, but there are moments that stand out as important milestones, like the bioluminescent algae that replaced electric fixtures, and the vast, subterranean mycelium network that triggered a new capacity for interspecies communication among buildings and animals—a development that expand-ed the agency, adaptability, and interactivity of ar-chitectural creatures. The subsequent transfor-mation of human economic systems generated another cascade of effects that revolutionized how we all spent our days, how we related to each other, and how we occupied and shared space. Once liberated from the myth of per-petual economic productivity, humans inte-grated the changes in their relationship with their homes that were initiated by the Great Pause. No longer burdened by the restless-ness of forced quarantine and nonstop work, the human-architecture symbiosis of home evolved into a camaraderie characterized by ease, play, and pleasure. In this new context, human children were granted new freedoms to define the activities of their everyday life outside of institutional frameworks. This is how I remember most of our life together.

You woke up close to me on the morning of your sixth birthday. You stood on your toes and put your ear against the vent. You could tell that your parents were still sleeping. "Just play quietly until we're up," they had told you the day before. But you didn't want to play—you wanted to be held. I tilted my torso against your bedroom wall and puffed out my belly to form a backrest and stoop. You nestled into my crevices and leaned your head into a well-positioned niche. We held on to each other as you yawned and flipped through the pages of your favorite book. Each of us breathed and waited.

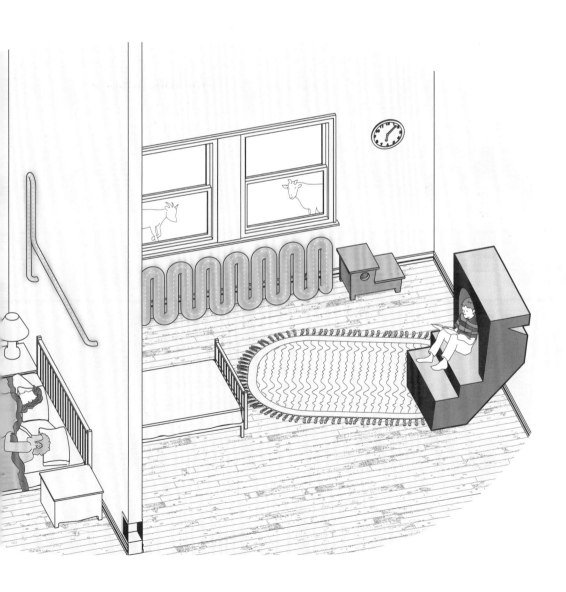

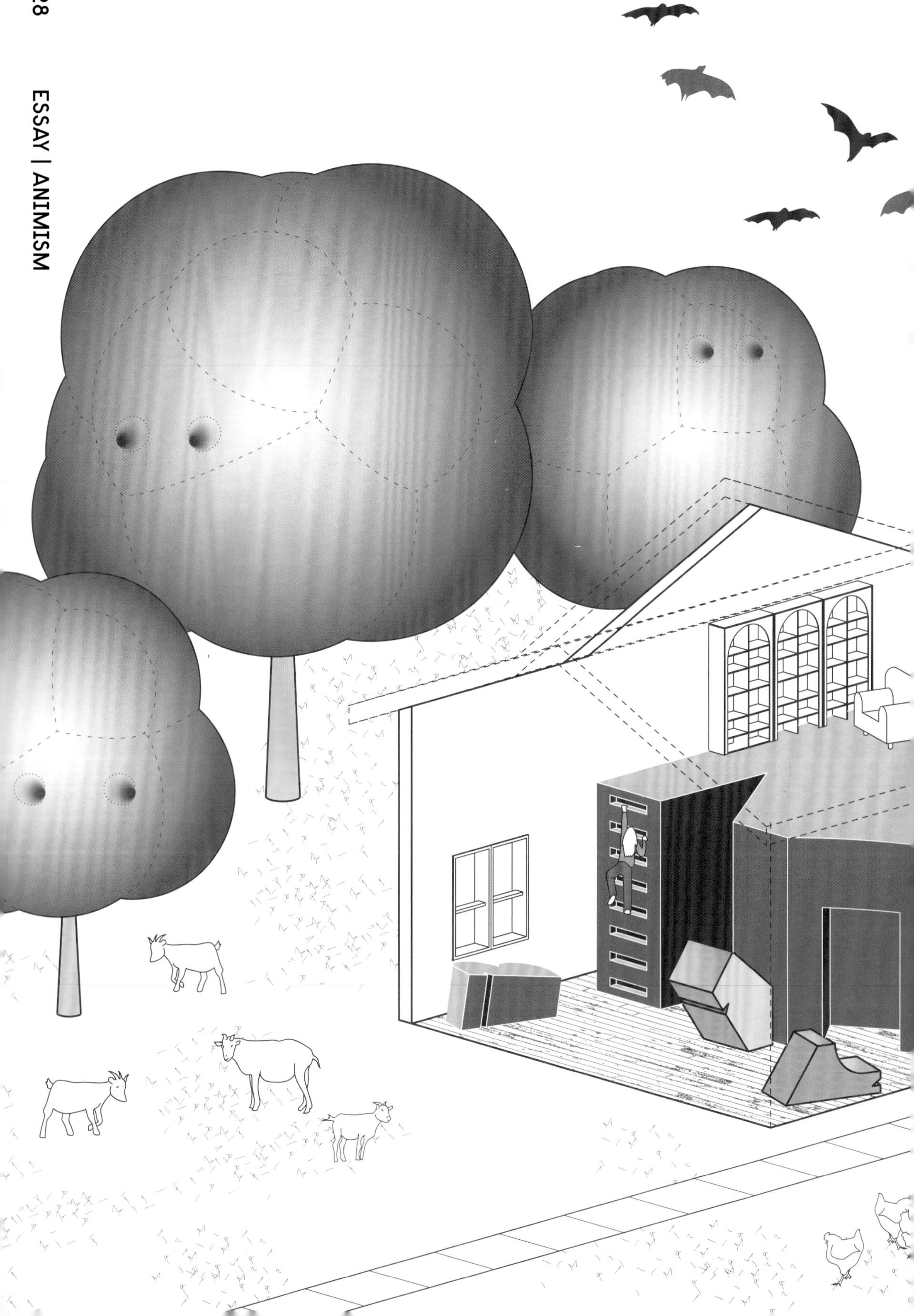

From the Balcony

The human liberation had a ripple effect across all the Kindoms of creatures. It was almost as if a spell had been broken. While it was too late to undo much of the irreparable harm, the massive cultural, social, and political paradigm shifts that occurred in less than a decade pulled the emergency brake on centuries of destructive habits and gave everyone a chance to take a long, deep breath. And on the exhale, we looked around and saw that while we each had our own distinct role to play in the rebuilding of the world, you and I had so much more in common than we had previously understood. With the reduced constraints of time and energy, we had space to explore the more subtle nuances of our relationship, and you started to see patterns in our relationship that mirrored the patterns of your relationships with your family members and friends, including the nonhuman "pets" and plants that you brought into us. You also became aware that the nonhumans, including buildings, formed their own bonds in relationships that existed outside of your influence. In the fluid and intimate configurations of kinship and affinity that we cultivated within our shared homes, between rooms and buildings and blocks and neighborhoods, we found new definitions of family, companionship, and citizenship.

I loved collaborations, but this one was different. I knew you loved her deeply, but what would that mean for me? I couldn't help but feel jealous of your romantic partnership—no one knows you better than me! What would her lifelong architectural companion think of me, and how would we all come together as a new family of four in this first home we all shared? It was a basic modular house, and

I could see her disappointment as she stepped through the front door. "It's missing so much," she grumbled. "It just needs…" And as she tapered off, you finished her sentence: "…character." When I heard this, I leaned over to our new architectural life partner and whispered in her ear: "Meet me at the back of the house." I wrapped my arcade to form a circular courtyard and stretched out a structural appendage for her to furnish a shapely balcony. In turn, she burrowed an oculus through the attic, letting in streams of warm evening sunlight and airborne companions. "This is better than I remember," she exclaimed, and we all had to agree. Each of us breathed and explored. ●

Solidarity, or How Architectural Creatures Love

Saved By The Whale: Dutch Train Runs Off Elevated Tracks, Is Caught By Statue's Tail

—NPR, November 2, 2020

Barcelona Opera Reopens With An Audience Of Plants

—NPR, June 22, 2020

Worlds are perforated and permeable, which is why we can share them....Worlds must be full of holes. Worlds malfunction intrinsically. All worlds are "poor"....This means that human worlds are not different in value from nonhuman ones, also that non-sentient nonhuman lifeforms...and non-life...also have worlds. Something like a permeable boundary between things and their phenomena is highly necessary for thinking solidarity.

—Timothy Morton

Figure 3.1. *Whale Tails* sculpture keeps derailed train aloft. Photo by Robin Utrecht/ANP/AFP via Getty Images.

The image of a train car teetering off the edge of an elevated platform is one we'd more likely expect to see on a poster for the next *Mission: Impossible* movie than in a real-life newspaper. When that train is perched on the tail of a whale, the scene takes a turn toward the even more surreal. Yet the meaning embedded in this image is all the more potent because its content is drawn not from an artist's imagination, but from an actual act of solidarity between humankind and an abiotic, creaturely sculpture: in this case, *Whale Tails,* a public work of art in the Netherlands that propped up a metro train that overran its stop in November 2020 (Figure 3.1). This uncanny event, which amplified the agency of an already animated zoomorphic structure, illustrates the solidarity this book aspires toward in making a case for creaturely architecture and reminds us that this rapport already exists in the world. Architecture does, in fact, save lives on a regular basis. When that architecture is in the form of a charismatic cetacean tail, we have an opportunity to anthropomorphize its service as an act of courage or compassion. And because we see ourselves reflected back in the forms that surround us, perhaps we also have a chance to see a little more courage or compassion in ourselves.

In June 2020, a slightly more sophisticated but equally surreal image sent a related message of solidarity under the headline "Barcelona Opera Reopens With An Audience Of Plants." In the midst of the COVID-19 pandemic, live performance spaces around the world suffered through indefinite closures. Venues adjusted to deliver cultural content through online platforms—but this substitute was incomplete for both audience members and performers, who thrive on the exchange of energy that is possible only in live events. In response to these circumstances, the artist Eugenio Ampudia installed 2,292 plants in the seats of the Barcelona Opera—the full capacity of the theater—to enjoy a performance of Giacomo Puccini's *Crisantemi* by a string quartet (Figure 3.2). The innovation at the Barcelona Opera granted access to culture to a wildly underrepresented portion of Earth's population: plant life.[1] The novelty of staring out into a sea of vegetation must have stirred a different kind of performative verve in the hearts of the musicians. Humans, formerly privileged audience members, may feel a twinge of jealousy seeing how easily plants can act as architecture's primary occupants. And as for the plants themselves, while it is harder to conceptualize what this opportunity for cultural engagement did for them emotionally, studies have shown that classical music stimulates plant growth, so it is likely that the

---

1   Rachel Treisman, "Barcelona Opera Reopens with an Audience of Plants," *NPR*, June 22, 2020, https://www.npr.org/sections/coronavirus-live-updates/2020/06/22/881943143/barcelona-opera-reopens-with-an-audience-of-plants.

Figure 3.2. Eugenio Ampudia, *Concert for the Biocence*, 2020. Photo courtesy of the artist.

experience stirred some good vibrations in their chloroplasts.[2]

Speaking of good vibrations, have you
ever seen nematode worms and rotifers get down together on the dance
floor? These microorganisms certainly
know a thing or two about rhythmic
wiggling, and according to the Queer
Ecologies Collective, the Microbe
Disco, held in August 2020, was an
opportunity to learn "from alter-life
how to do joy, how to do pleasure,
how to do interdependence, how to
dance" (Figure 3.3). The virtual event
featured a live stream of a compost
heap under a microscope "where

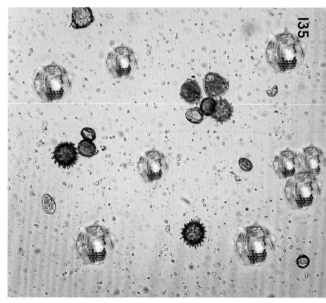

Figure 3.3. Linden K. MacMahon, *Microbe Disco*, 2020.

bacteria, and amoeba jiggle and twist with one another, digesting waste materials,
making vibrations and busting moves"; "as things get moving," the event description
explains, "other creatures arrive, including worms, woodlice, rotifers, arthropods and
humans."[3] As an intervention to help overcome the isolation, grief, and rage of quarantine, *and* to stand against climate colonialism with and for the nonhuman portion
of our population by making the invisible visible, the Microbe Disco advanced the
mission of Queer Ecologies Collective to tell "new stories about nature and our connection to it, empowering interspecies collaborations, and honouring the inherently
queer patterns and relations found throughout nature."[4] For its human participants,
the event was a healthy reminder that some of the best dance parties in the world
take place in discos the size of a petri dish.

Each of these examples demonstrates how animate architectural elements—
whether sculptural ornament, proscenium seating, or a microscope and disco
ball—can facilitate forms of interspecies interactions that challenge conventional
notions of the separation between human life and "nature." These three examples
are among the more evocative instances in a wider trend of stories, memes, and
online events that expressed and celebrated one of the most profound revelations
in the early days of the coronavirus pandemic in the spring of 2020: a collective
desire to reconnect with "nature" and reintroduce it into cities. Many found a silver

2   See, for example, Emran Khan Chowdhury, Hyoun-Sub Lim, and Hanhong Bae, "Update on the Effects of
    Sound Wave on Plants," *Research in Plant Disease* 20, no. 1 (2014): 1–7. *Crisantemi* translates to chry-
    santhemums—a choice that perhaps deepened the connection.
3   "Queer Ecologies: Microbe Disco," Phytology, accessed April 11, 2021, https://phytology.org.uk/calen-
    dar/queer-ecologies-microbe-disco/.
4   "Microbe Disco," Electric Dreams Online, accessed April 11, 2021, https://electricdreamsfestival.com/
    microbedisco/.

lining of the quarantine in images of nature's "return" to city centers brought to a standstill by the lockdown. Anecdotes proliferated, some real and some fake, with headlines like "Emboldened wild animals venture into locked-down cities worldwide" and "Venice canals run clear, dolphins appear in Italy's waterways amid coronavirus lockdown" and tweets about dinosaurs returning to Central Park.

But the giddy proclamations also revealed a misguided naivete about the nature of our relationship to nature, specifically a critical misinterpretation of our separateness from it. In order to correct this general misunderstanding, Timothy Morton substitutes the term "nature" with the idea of the "symbiotic real," "a weird 'implosive whole' in which entities are related in a non-total, ragged way." In his book *Humankind: Solidarity with Nonhuman People*, Morton makes the case for an updated version of Marxist communism that "only works when its economic models are thought as an attunement to the fact of living in a biosphere."[5] This revision argues for a version of solidarity that is based on a new understanding of what it is to "have in common." For Morton, solidarity is easier, or "cheaper," than one might expect, because it is a fact of ecological existence that does not require human thought or feeling to make it so.[6] For humans, this easy solidarity may be the basis of new forms of companionship with architecture and other beings. As we see in the examples above, this can include being saved by architecture, replaced by plants, or decentered by microscopic organisms.

SOLIDARITY AND COLLECTIVES

Only through solidarity can we get ourselves out of this collective prison. Memes save lives.

—Instagram post by @dank.lloyd.wright[7]

Office Kovacs's *Proposal for Collective Living II (Homage to Sir John Soane)*, exhibited at the 2017 Chicago Architecture Biennial, is an architectural model of a speculative cityscape that "conceptually turns Soane's House inside out."[8] It arranges an assortment of plastic ready-made components—architectural elements from modeling kits and toys such as bridges, plants, animals, figures, and landforms—into a multi-tiered, interconnected, and nonhierarchical matrix that operates at a range of scales and orientations (Figure 3.4). For a scenario that defies laws of nature defining our existing realities, with the overall appearance of a kitbashed fun house, the proposal has a surprising plausibility. Although the whole world of this proposal may seem unruly, the smaller, intimate moments where a

5   Morton, *Humankind*, 1.

6   Morton, 13–14.

7   @dank.lloyd.wright, "Only through solidarity can we get ourselves out of this collective prison. Memes save lives," Instagram post.

8   "Chicago Model," Office Kovacs, accessed April 19, 2021, https://o-k-o-k.net/CHICAGO-MODEL.

Figure 3.4. Office Kovacs, *Proposal for Collective Living II (Homage to Sir John Soane)*, 2017.

human figure confronts the two or three nearest elements in their vicinity (such as a ceiling-mounted fire hydrant or an oversized rubber duck atop a pile of bricks) prod us to suspend our disbelief and to immerse ourselves in the strange familiarity of this urban context. The relationships that congeal in these discrete parts start to tell stories that draw us into the model's worldmaking, despite its anarchic lack of legibility and absurdity as a whole.

Office Kovacs's model is an embodiment of the symbiotic real that Morton describes. The heaps of colorful objects are tied together in a range of relational combinations, but its wholeness is less important than the character of its individual parts. In its apparent chaos, all parts share a unity in their equivalent opportunity to be read at any given moment as either focal points of a captivating narrative or background noise in the web of interrelated elements.

In Morton's conception of the symbiotic real, all things and beings coexist as interrelated entities whose boundaries are permeable and ambiguous. While every thing or being has distinct qualities of its own, each also comprises aggregations of parts that in themselves have their own distinct qualities, and that exist in symbiosis with other things or beings to compose larger wholes. Morton articulates this fact with a clever and counterintuitive twist on a familiar phrase: "a whole is always *less* than the sum of its parts," a phenomenon he refers to as "subscendence."[9] In

Figure 3.5. Dank Lloyd Wright, Instagram post, 2020. Screenshot by authors.

Proposal for Collective Living II, architectural objects, including ladders, fences, columns, and windows, define spaces as individual parts, but they operate equally as subsets of mini-environments (balconies, veranda, and catwalks) as well as larger groups of complexes and interiors. Each part, subset, and permutation of space-making is just as real an architectural environment as the whole world, so the parts exceed the whole in number, qualities, and identity.

The manipulation and reconfiguration of part-to-whole relationships is a fundamental strategy in every architect's bag of tricks, and therefore a useful point of entry for the world of architecture into the subscendence of the symbiotic real and the philosophical language of *Humankind.* Architecture operates as both a collection of parts and a discrete object (a pile of bricks, for example), but also a more elusive "space between" that cannot always be apprehended discretely (it is all around us all the time; it is connected to organisms, ecologies, infrastructures, economies, and systems of power). As an object, architecture plays a critical role in the definition of boundaries that establish guidelines for inclusion and exclusion, and by extension identity, agency, and citizenship. Yet simultaneously, the products of architecture are participants in those relational dynamics, subject to the warmth of belonging as well as the sting of alienation. This tension between object and field, autonomy and interconnectedness, terminal uniqueness and background noise, is something that we, as humans, have in common with architecture. To acknowledge that shared experience is a version of solidarity that is within reach. Creaturely architectures are beings with the capacity to navigate between the desire to be recognized as a legible whole, and the impulse to be one small part of something bigger.

The meme collective Dank Lloyd Wright (DLW) enacts a similar methodology of crafting surprisingly plausible parts in relation to a seemingly unruly but symbiotic whole—though in their case as a project of "emerging" architectural theory as opposed to speculative design. Unlike other recent efforts in architectural meme-making by single authors, Dank Lloyd Wright is produced by (or appears to be produced by) a variegated yet coordinated "hivemind" of "admins" who each offer unique styles, affinities, and tones of voice, but share a common disciplinary and political agenda. Here, single social media posts deliver the parts, or stand-alone memes, but collective recurring themes, recursive references, and deliberate narrative arcs across these disparate posts shape an ongoing story about the kind of architecture (and architects) that they want to see (or don't want to see) in the world.

In a whopping fifteen posts per day on average, the prolific, anonymous collective makes architectural jokes as commentary (and commentary as jokes) that "demolish the white male Eurocentric architectural canon and help rewrite history with accuracy and representation and remove rapists, snake oil salesmen, and shameless grifters while we are at it."[10] As of this writing, DLW has 36,000 followers and counting, a number that spawns copious commenting and digital interactions among its dedicated global audiences. A single meme might be fleeting and forgettable, but a barrage of casual-seeming but highly coordinated messaging over a sustained period of time yields a radical shift in architectural discourse and culture that constitutes a generational movement. DLW acknowledges that memes are the medium of the moment, and that when instrumentalized by a disciplined commitment to collective solidarity, the seemingly innocuous or frivolous gesture is translated into an accessible, game-changing delivery system for a new species of architectural theory.

Like memes and internet ephemera in general,[11] creatures and creatureliness play a prominent and recurring role in DLW's content and span the categories of zoomorphism, animism, and solidarity that compose this book. For instance, on June 10, 2020, DLW posted an image of the Dog Bark Park Inn, a hound-shaped bed and breakfast in Cottonwood, Idaho, with a caption reading "Fuck wasn't supposed to post this please delete??"—as if one admin accidentally revealed their guilty pleasure of "animal replica" architecture to the hivemind (Figure 3.5).[12] The staged embarrassment of liking a beagle building is a reminder of the

---

10   Quoted in Giovanni Comoglio, "Just What Is It That Makes Memes So Different, So Appealing?," *Domus*, July 20, 2020, https://www.domusweb.it/en/architecture/gallery/2020/07/09/memes-or-it-didnt-happen.html.

11   One particular creature, the cat, has a special place on the internet: "images and videos of domestic cats make up some of the most viewed content on the web, particularly image macros in the form of lolcats. ThoughtCatalog has described cats as the 'unofficial mascot of the Internet'." Wikipedia, s.v. "Cats and the Internet," last modified April 6, 2021, https://en.wikipedia.org/wiki/Cats_and_the_Internet.

12   @dank.lloyd.wright, Instagram, June 10, 2020.

unacceptability of blatant zoomorphism (or kitsch and playfulness in general) in a canon steeped in anthropocentric anthropomorphism and self-seriousness, and calls into question which powers in architecture do and should enjoy the privilege of being arbiters of taste and validity.

In another post, the meme shows a stock photo of a white guy "listening" to a brick wall, with a speech bubble voicing the question, "Hey brick, what do you want to be someday?"[13] The brick responds, cheekily, "Call your wife Louis." As a censure upon the whole discipline for idolizing a patriarchal, sexist white man as an architectural hero, this meme also celebrates an animist perspective, one through which buildings have the capacity not only to communicate, but also to put humans in their place. Louis Kahn may have asked a brick what it wanted as a parable for his own architectural or pedagogical agenda, but DLW imagines a future where architectural matter has existential agency to decenter human privilege and dismantle clout.

In turn, DLW embodies a new mode of architectural theory and criticism that propels solidarity on multiple levels. On one level, DLW's content argues for another world of architectural labor and livelihood based on creaturely solidarity that is rid of capitalist labor abuses and exploitative "starchitect" culture. On another, DLW's mode of narration is enacted through a "hivemind" solidarity of authors who may sport different affinities (e.g., "plan gang" versus "section gang") but who articulate a common goal for the architectural masses.

---

13   @dank.lloyd.wright, Instagram post, 2020.

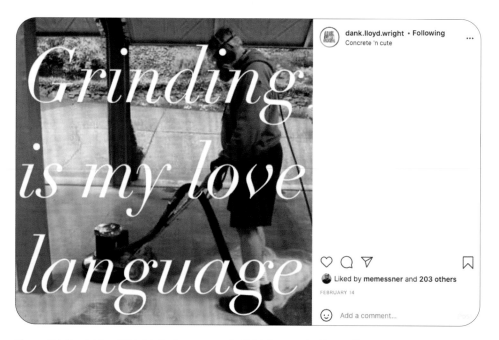

Figure 3.6. Dank Lloyd Wright, Instagram post, 2021. Screenshot by authors.

EXPANDING PERSONHOOD

In the previous two essays, we put forward formal and organizational strategies that render individual architectural projects capable of looking like and behaving like animate creatures. In this section, we look at the collective impact of a creaturely architecture that operates from a position of solidarity with other creaturely beings in the world (human, nonhuman, and abiotic) by offering strategies to feel "in common" with the built environment and its various inhabitants. If our short-term goals include the production of zoomorphic and animated characters whose friendly affects contribute to a playful environment of camaraderie and joy, the long game for such projects liberates architecture's cultural production from the constraints of a worldview that is confined by terms set according to the demands of capitalism and dominated by ego and self-promotion. What does it mean if we take ourselves, our architecture, or our human privilege a little less seriously, just enough to make space for other forms of beings? Our proposed outcome is an architectural culture that can simultaneously acknowledge the responsibility that comes with its inherent agency and retain a sense of humor, compassion, and willingness to honor the agency of other participants in the process of design, including the output of the design process itself. Perhaps it looks a little something like the world of Dank Lloyd Wright. To give the end products of architecture (including theory and criticism) a life of their own, to see them as animate characters with personality and agency, is to relinquish an element of control by granting architecture, and the ambiguous collective that nurtures it, the status of personhood.

Recently, there has been a changing of attitudes about the meaning of "personhood," a status that has expanded in scientific and legal contexts to characterize a broader array of nonhuman others, such as certain animals and natural resources. Granting personhood to these entities assures and defends their rights to existence and protection. In 2014, for example, the government of India recognized dolphins as nonhuman persons, citing their intelligence and self-awareness as a justification to ban practices that keep them in captivity or use them for entertainment.[14] In 2019, the people of Toledo, Ohio, voted to grant personhood to Lake Erie, a measure meant to protect their major source of drinking water from ongoing agricultural and industrial contamination; as *Smithsonian Magazine* reported, "Lake Erie can thus 'stand' to sue polluters (with a little help from human attorneys, of course)."[15]

While these developments are promising steps forward for the environmental movement, the definition of personhood as a mechanism to grant "rights" to

---

14   Saroja Coelho, "Dolphins Gain Unprecedented Protection in India," *Deutsche Welle*, May 24, 2013. https://www.dw.com/en/dolphins-gain-unprecedented-protection-in-india/a-16834519.

15   Jason Daley, "Toledo, Ohio, Just Granted Lake Erie the Same Legal Rights as People," *Smithsonian*, March 1, 2019, https://www.smithsonianmag.com/smart-news/toledo-ohio-just-granted-lake-erie-same-legal-rights-people-180971603/.

exceptional bodies (of mammals or water) stops far short of embracing the full enactment of identity and agency that personhood implies. We have more in common with a river, a centipede, a toy centipede, a rock, a table, or a building than a traditional Western worldview acknowledges. Beyond preventing harm (such as captivity or contamination), loosening the requirements for nonhuman personhood might also enable new pleasures. Discouraging anthropocentric violence is one thing, but transforming an anthropocentric worldview in which humans extract and dominate "resources" into a worldview that establishes a shared footing for humans and nonhumans initiates a new world in which nonhuman others can affect humans as companion creatures. What if Lake Erie's standing waters could teach us a new way to stand (and feel)? What if we could share an emotional bond with the brick bond composing the masonry walls of our home?

It may be possible to feel this kind of connection with any form of built structure, regardless of material, form, or context; however, we suspect that creaturely architectures, which display some combination of zoomorphism, animism, and solidarity, can operate as didactic tools that ease us into these relationships by endowing architecture with relatable qualities that make interaction more accessible and

Figure 3.7. Chris T. Cornelius (studio:indigenous), *Domicile_02: Maple Syrup Moon*.

plausible. Storytelling is one of the more effective points of entry for empathy and engagement with another being, human or nonhuman. Chris T. Cornelius of studio:indigenous describes himself as a storyteller who creates characters through drawing and design. A citizen of the Oneida Nation, he translates the oral traditions of his cultural heritage through architectural projects such as his series *Moon Domicile* (Figure 3.7). Each dwelling in the series is composed of a set of architectural elements whose geometries are constrained by the wind patterns of each cycle of the Oneida moon calendar. "The architectural elements that I play with are; the legs; where the dwelling meets the sky; the way in; the ground it sits on; the modulation of light via cantilevers—each of these present a representational opportunity. I would like the viewer to see them and wonder if it smells, or sweats, or ambulates," Cornelius writes. "These forms show up as protective carapace, supportive structures, water collection wings, support columns, canopy/headdress, and projective subtraction."[16] The context in which these structures sit is spare—ground, sky, wind pattern diagram, and a creaturely scale figure (bear, wolf, dear, hedgehog) are all that accompanies each structure. Yet Cornelius's compositions of architectural features, appendages, and gestures are in dynamic dialogue with these contextual companions, and through this dialogue each composition tells a different story about the character of the domicile that the drawing represents.

We might adopt architecture as a fellow person among other nonhuman companions we relate to in the plant and animal kingdoms (perhaps even adding a kingdom of architecture onto the existing biological classification system). While legal protections granted to building "persons" may be as instrumental for architecture as they may prove to be for our biological counterparts (or corporations, for that matter), we are even more interested in architectural personhood as a prompt to form relationships with buildings, expanding the greater human capacity for solidarity—a state of empathy, kindred, and friendship. And if we can cultivate pleasurable friendships with our buildings, perhaps we can also amplify our capacity to empathize with humans different from ourselves. On the other hand, our solidarity with these architectures may be accompanied by their own enhanced agency to reject our companionship, or at least to push it aside in order to prioritize the subjecthood of some other being. Nevertheless, this kind of vulnerability is always the risk when opening oneself up to relationships with other creatures.

CREATURELY CITIZENS: LEARNING FROM CHILDREN

If it feels daunting or unrealistic, or even frivolous, to imagine the solidarity that we have been describing, then perhaps we might look more closely at the lives and behaviors of children to remember how easy and important it can be. The scholar

---

16   "Domicile Series," studio:indigenous, accessed April 27, 2021, https://www.studioindigenous.com/domicile-series.

of education and pedagogy Jane Merewether theorizes how the "enchanted an-imism" embodied by children helps to dispel the notion that seeing and embracing the animate nature of things is a symptom of primitive thinking. Challenging the psychologist Jean Piaget's interpretation of children's animism as a primitive de-velopmental stage that we leave behind to become rational adults, Merewether argues that "children's playful-yet-serious animism provides a bridge between the immobilising emotions of hope and despair that dominate in a world of unprece-dented challenges. ...It is a speculative move that requires invention and imagina-tion, but it is also deeply rooted in experience."[17] This practice of speculative play is not fanciful escapism or ignorant naivete, but rather its opposite: it is an expression of children's capacity for presence, and their willingness to experience surprise and wonder as they take in the world without the filter of preconceived ideas, definitions, and classifications. This openness that exists in the moment before we name something, or put it in a box of predetermined meaning, is the underpinning of the bridge that allows for the fluid navigation between hope and despair, pre-cisely because those conditions have yet to be labeled as good or bad.

Furthermore, Merewether posits that this experience of animism is something from which the adult world could learn, emphasizing its implications for an expand-ed ethic of care: "Children's lively views of the world...opened a space of caring human–non human and entirely abiotic non human relations. [Their] playful and speculative animism...decentred the human and offered a way to see the non human world as more than mute resources that are there for the taking." Within this space of mutual care we also find a space of political co-creation: "[Animism] can offer a space of encounter in which humans and non humans might come together in ways that 'invite the risk of response' and opportunities for 'pro-voking political and ethical imagination in the present,'" she writes, quoting the scholars Donna Haraway and Maria Puig de la Bellacasa.[18] This is the space that a creaturely architecture supports, nurtures, and occupies in the production of new worlds. However, there is much for architecture to unlearn before it can step into its agency to operate in this mode. Piaget suggested that children naturally develop out of their innate animism, but the fact is that we are taught out of it. As Robin Wall Kimmerer observes in *Braiding Sweetgrass*, "The animacy of the world is something we already know, but the language of animacy teeters on extinction. ...Our toddlers speak of plants and animals as if they were people...until we teach them not to. We quickly retrain them and make them forget. When we tell them that the tree is not a who, but an it, we make that maple an object. ...Saying it makes a living land into 'natural resources.'"[19] Similarly, when we are taught that

---

17   Jane Merewether, "Enchanted Animism: A Matter of Care," *Contemporary Issues in Early Childhood* (November 2020): 4, https://doi.org/10.1177%2F1463949120971380.

18   Merewether, 9.

19   Robin Wall Kimmerer, *Braiding Sweetgrass: Indigenous Wisdom, Scientific Knowledge, and the Teach-ings of Plants* (Minneapolis, MN: Milkweed Editions, 2013), 57.

the building is not a who, but an it, a living building becomes a mute service provider and we lose an opportunity to encounter another being with imagination and a mutual interest in creating a different future.

The dynamics of care between children, adults, nonhumans, and built structures is a prominent theme of the 2012 film *Beasts of the Southern Wild,* which was cowritten and directed by Benh Zeitlin. The film is a contemporary allegory that represents the near-future symbiotic realness and solidarity of a small island community in the Gulf Coast living under imminent threat from regular and soon to be permanent flooding. Their community has been nicknamed "The Bathtub" because it is located on the "wrong" side of the levees that simultaneously protect a nearby city and exacerbate flooding on their island. Human inhabitants of the Bathtub are centered as the protagonists, yet their lives are deeply intertwined with those of the water, trees, animals, boats, and buildings with whom they share the world, and which are at risk of being destroyed when the next big storm rolls in. Five-year-old Hushpuppy and her father, Wink, are among a determined crowd of island-dwellers who live in ad hoc, stilted, and armored creature-like structures, eat meals from piles of freshly caught shellfish, poured straight from the net onto a shared table, celebrate life with parades and fireworks on any given day, and drink themselves unconscious when an impending storm threatens another flood. There is an understandable tension between residents of the Bathtub and the Federal Emergency Management Agency authorities from the adjacent city who are forcing evacuation of their home island, a tension still unresolved by the end of the film.

In the film's first scenes, Hushpuppy wanders around her yard picking up young chicks and listening to their heartbeats. She narrates the interaction in voice-over: "All the time, everywhere, everything's hearts are beating and squirting, and talking to each other in ways I can't understand. Most of the time they probably be saying: I'm hungry, or I gotta poop, but sometimes they be talking in codes." This is a practice that Hushpuppy will repeat throughout the film—listening to the heartbeats of domesticated animals, trees, fish, and sometimes fellow humans—as she attempts to provide care that she may or may not be equipped to provide. Nevertheless, this practice provides clues to the lessons that we might learn from her ability to navigate the bridge that Merewether describes between despair and hope. Hushpuppy lives in fear of becoming meat to mythical aurochs, creatures stampeding south through her imagination upon release from the melting ice caps to the north. In the final scenes of the movie, Hushpuppy has the opportunity to confront these beasts face-to-face, and hearing their heartbeats, learns to see them as companions, beasts in solidarity as they confront the end of the world as they collectively know it.

Kyo Maclear's 2018 analysis and critique of the film and its reception acknowledges the film's accomplishments: "*Beasts* is many films. It is an ecological fairy tale and a rising seas story. It is a tale of a multiracial community and precarious freedom. It is a story of girlhood survival, and of what it means to come to terms with mortality, in the face of personal and planetary disasters."[20] Its representation of the beauty and magic of a troubled world from the nonpatronizing vantage point of a child, as well as its illustration of a value system that prioritizes joy, connection, and solidarity above material comforts, offers its audience a chance not only to see the world from a perspective not often seen or heard in a mainstream American culture, but also to reckon with the potential contradictions that exist within those underrepresented perspectives. Yet Maclear emphasizes how important it is to address those contradictions: "Ideas of resilience need to be responsive to longstanding histories of structural violence and neglect. Expectations of grit and tenacity without a functional infrastructure of care (however incomplete and impossible) risk perpetuating abandonment and

---

20   Kyo Maclear, "Something So Broken: Black Care in the Wake of Beasts of the Southern Wild," *ISLE: Interdisciplinary Studies in Literature and Environment* 25, no. 3 (Summer 2018): 608.

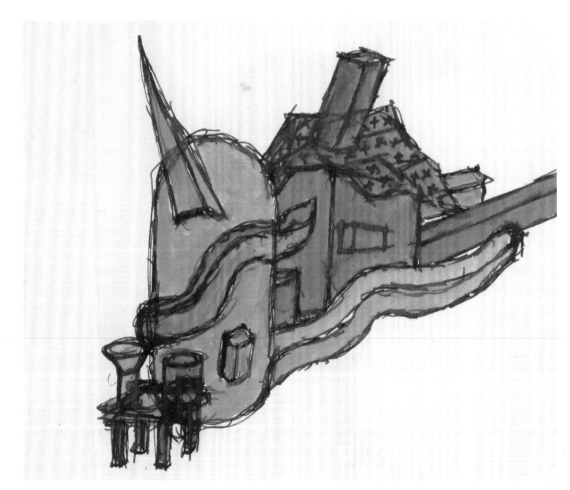

Figure 3.8. John Hejduk, Sketch from *Architectures in Love*, 1994. John Hejduk fonds, Canadian Centre for Architecture © CCA.

injustice."[21] Despite, or perhaps because of, the film's shortcomings, it is possible to learn from Zeitlin's effort to locate, in a child's perspective, the nascent impulse in aspects of Western culture to see outside of an anthropocentric worldview. Yet in the failed efforts to embrace these connections that we have not yet given ourselves the chance to cultivate, we also identify the systemic forces that keep such impulses in check. We look to both the triumphs of Hushpuppy and the failures of the systems around her as guidance. She is a figure whose alchemical powers come from a willingness to immerse herself in the relational dynamics of her world, to swim in the murky and dangerous waters of her circumstances, and to improvise her way through challenges by working with and learning from the people, buildings, objects, and environments in which she finds herself. However, the power of her imagination and grit is not sufficient if she is not supported by a collective network of care that can match her capacity for solidarity and love. Hushpuppy's power comes not from slaying the monsters who threaten her worlds, but rather by turning them into friends in order to defuse their threat. In the case of architecture, humans might be the monster whose dominance can be subverted by giving some creaturely agency to the process and product with which we engage—and a new language of solidarity and love might transmute our potential threat and create a new collective endeavor of world-building.

SPECTRUMS OF SOLIDARITY: THE LOVE LANGUAGES OF CREATURES

> Grammar is just the way we chart relationships in language. Maybe it also reflects our relationships with each other. Maybe a grammar of animacy could lead us to whole new ways of living in the world, other species a sovereign people, a world with a democracy of species, not a tyranny of one.
>
> —Robin Wall Kimmerer[22]

The commonality, connection, empathy, and vulnerability that accompany solidarity are often also described as qualities of love. *Love* is a word that is conspicuously absent from most architectural discourse. John Hejduk published a sketchbook, titled *Architectures in Love*, that depicts zoomorphic building forms engaged in sexual intercourse or otherwise expressing physical affection and "tenderness" with one another (Figure 3.8).[23] While we celebrate buildings engaging in consensual pleasure to consummate their buildingly love, this series of illustrations is perhaps more allegorical than literal. In order to develop an expanded vocabulary of architectural love, we turn to Gary Chapman's best-selling book *The Five Love Languages: How to Express Heartfelt Commitment to Your Mate* for some guidance.

21   Maclear, 608.
22   Kimmerer, *Braiding Sweetgrass*, 57–58.
23   John Hejduk, *Architectures In Love* (New York: Rizzoli, 1995).

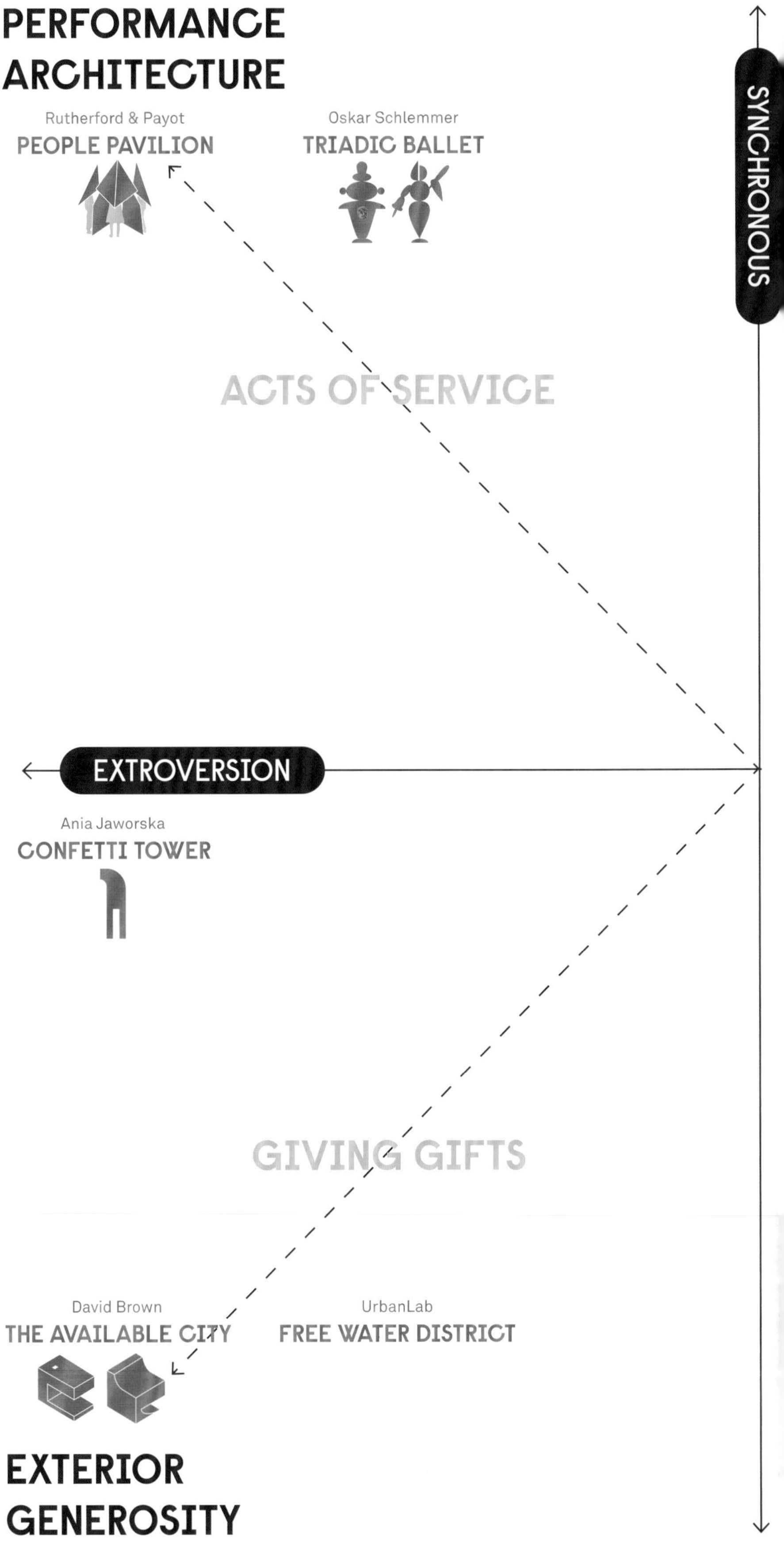

PERFORMANCE ARCHITECTURE

Rutherford & Payot
PEOPLE PAVILION

Oskar Schlemmer
TRIADIC BALLET

ACTS OF SERVICE

←—— **EXTROVERSION** ——

Ania Jaworska
CONFETTI TOWER

GIVING GIFTS

David Brown
THE AVAILABLE CITY

UrbanLab
FREE WATER DISTRICT

EXTERIOR GENEROSITY

SYNCHRONOUS

**Figure 3.9.
Solidarity
Matrix.**

HOW ARCHITECTURAL CREATURES LOVE

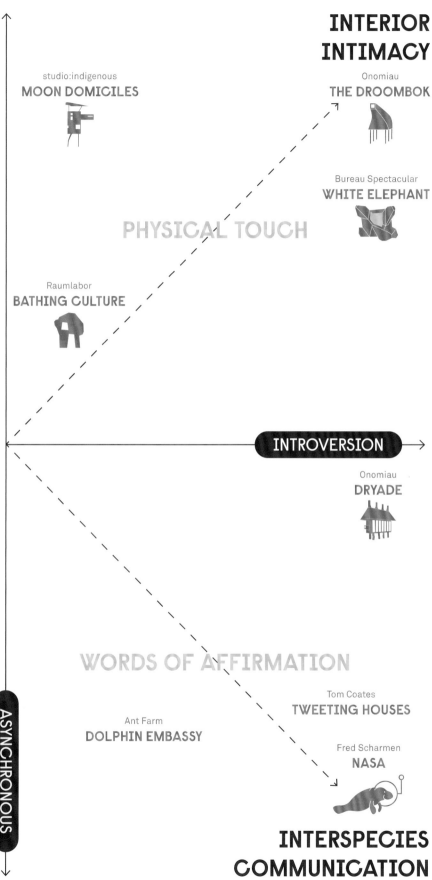

INTERIOR INTIMACY

studio:indigenous
MOON DOMICILES

Onomiau
THE DROOMBOK

Bureau Spectacular
WHITE ELEPHANT

PHYSICAL TOUCH

Raumlabor
BATHING CULTURE

INTROVERSION

Onomiau
DRYADE

WORDS OF AFFIRMATION

Tom Coates
TWEETING HOUSES

Ant Farm
DOLPHIN EMBASSY

Fred Scharmen
NASA

INTERSPECIES COMMUNICATION

The love languages codify the different ways humans express love.[24] When the love is interspecies or architectural, the communication gap has the potential to be even greater. Conveniently, four of Chapman's five love languages—words of affirmation, acts of service, physical touch, receiving gifts, and quality time—can be directly translated and applied to the series of creaturely architectural case studies discussed below, and located on the matrix shown in Figure 3.9.

Interspecies communication is a love language that is likely familiar if you live with and converse with a pet. Even if we can't understand the exact meaning of the nonhuman sounds that our pets (and our buildings!) utter on a regular basis, we can interpret the tone, tempo, inflection, and body language that accompany otherwise foreign expressions. Conversely, even if our nonhuman counterparts can't understand our human language, the act of expressing ourselves or confiding in them can reverberate and translate in unexpected ways among our nonhuman others. The love language of interspecies communication is located in a quadrant of the matrix defined by introversion and asynchronicity. On one hand, our words are an expression of our innermost feelings and experiences, and yet the translation across species implies a lag time in transmission and an indirect exchange from one being to the next, one that can sometimes take place across great expanses of both space and time.

Performance architecture is a love language delivered through action and animation. Unlike words of affirmation, this love language is extroverted and synchronous: it privileges what we do over what we say, it puts us out into the world with big, visible gestures, and it requires full presence in the moment. While we may regularly engage in routine, maintenance-oriented "acts of service" with the buildings we inhabit, what if we recast "housekeeping" as creative choreography of companion-keeping? By stepping into character and role-play, by donning costumes and accessories, and by sometimes just breaking into a little dance, we can relate with our built environment, and the creatures we share it with, in more loving ways.

Interior intimacy also requires the immediacy of deeply focused presence, but in a quiet, inwardly focused manner that we characterize as synchronous introversion. When we can simply be in close physical proximity to another body to exchange energy, to be held, to feel at one with a beloved, then there is no need for words or actions. In biological terms the closest physical intimacy we might experience is inside the womb of our mother. The architectural equivalent is the tender closeness we feel in a cozy, creaturely interior, one whose scale, atmosphere, and seclusion makes us feel protected and cared for in the most fundamental of ways.

---

24   Gary Chapman, *The Five Love Languages: How to Express Heartfelt Commitment to Your Mate* (Chicago: Northfield, 1992).

Exterior generosity advocates for urban environments that consider the shared experiences of all their inhabitants, including future generations who are not yet around to advocate for themselves. As an extroverted and asynchronous endeavor, the planning and design of cities that can integrate immediate needs and desires of grassroots organizing with long-term visionary strategies requires a generous spirit that is open to listening, processing, working, and sometimes disagreeing with as many different perspectives as possible.

INTERSPECIES COMMUNICATION

Many say that communication is key to any loving relationship, and this is especially true for architectural relationships. Humans have traditionally used architecture as a form of visual communication; the formal languages of architecture convey meaning through style, symbolism, abstraction, and graphics. Architects themselves communicate their ideas through drawings, in a range of contexts and formats. However, these communication techniques require a different approach when the dialogue is taking place between humans and nonhumans, or between humans and the buildings themselves.

The love languages of interspecies communication are the foundation of interspecies solidarity, and one of their most remarkable qualities is that they can transmit across great distances. Fred Scharmen's *Nonhuman Autonomous Space Agency* (*NASA*) launches communities of live animals and robotic creatures into low Earth orbit. This speculative version of NASA continues the lineage of early experiments in space travel in which dogs, monkeys, and rabbits were sent into space and subsequently returned to Earth. This time, however, a semi-aquatic habitat created within a hollow asteroid is sent into orbit for manatees

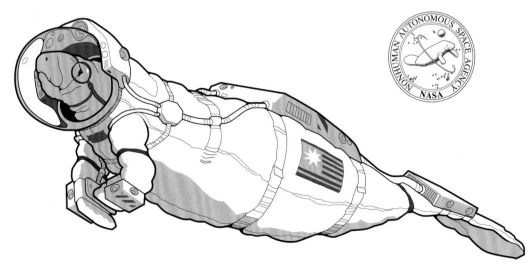

Figure 3.10. Fred Scharmen with the Working Group on Adaptive Systems, *Anatoly, Nonhuman Autonomous Space Agency*, 2015.

and chickens to inhabit and explore. The exploits and interactions of the space-bound animals are carefully monitored by autonomous robots, who digitally broadcast the animals' activities to an emerging public of Earth-dwelling human fans. In this way, *NASA* amplifies the subjectivity of these nonhuman astronauts (both animals and robots), giving them comprehensible and emotional voices understood by humans via the likes of Twitter.

As Scharmen explains, the project leverages the communicative power of charismatic megafauna, "a species of animal that is well known and well liked, which serves as a stand-in and focal point for the complexities of the ecosystem in which it lives." For example, manatees have come to serve as a mascot for water and habitat conservation because of their relatable anthropomorphic expressions and postures, which prompt empathetic responses from humans: "Talking about manatees is a way to begin to talk about how we use the landscape of Florida and the Caribbean recreationally, and how to possibly change some careless habits associated with that use."[25]

The project operates via two prominent drawings. The first introduces us to Anatoly, a manatee in a space suit, captured in the familiar pose and uniform of a human astronaut floating in space (Figure 3.10). The representational technique of line drawing heightens the manatee's character; the carefully composed wrinkles and expression on its face, visible through the helmet, convey confidence, curiosity, and even wisdom. This is a manatee with agency, and aspires to be a revamped Vitruvian nonhuman person for our time. The second drawing depicts a cross-section of the hollow ovoid orbital habitat (Figure 3.11). This strange diorama grants its resident creatures free

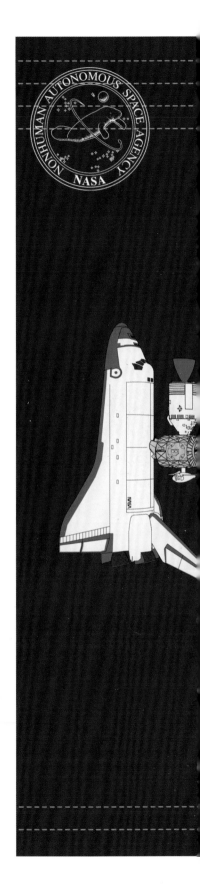

25   Fred Scharmen, "The Nonhuman Autonomous Space Agency," in *103rd ACSA Annual Meeting Paper Proceedings*, ed. Lola Sheppard and David Ruy (Washington, DC: ACSA Press, 2015), 500.

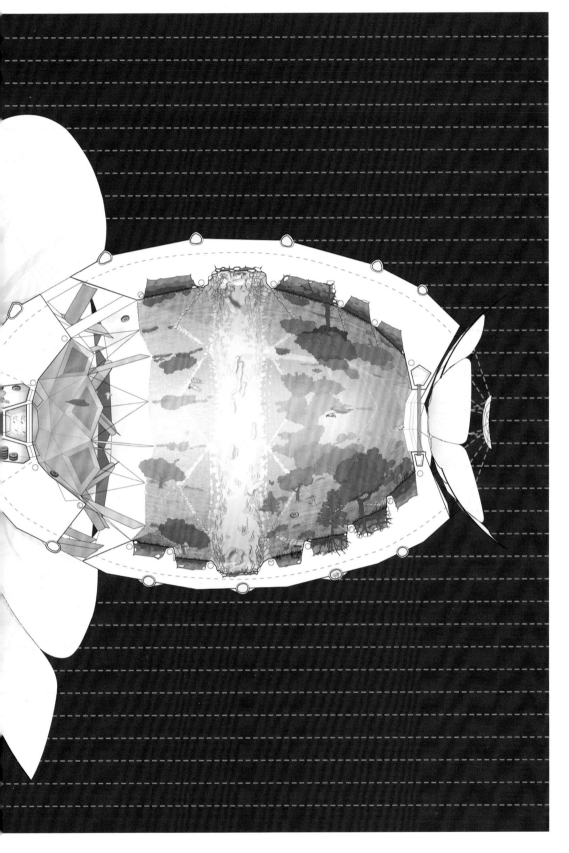

Figure 3.11. Fred Scharmen with the Working Group on Adaptive Systems, Section Detail, The Lazy River, *Nonhuman Autonomous Space Agency,* 2015.

rein to inhabit and occupy the artificial rural landscape carved into the asteroid interior, while human participation is limited to retweets and "likes" from afar. This model reminds human earthlings that they may not be the center of the universe after all. This is not necessarily to allow humans to relinquish their responsibility to "save the planet," but rather to champion the agency of nonhuman actors in the complex ecological workings of our world(s).

In his writing, Scharmen also examines the activities and perspectives of (earth-bound) houses with Twitter feeds that "give a voice to things that would otherwise be unable to communicate clearly to humans,"[26] and considers the implications for architectural communication when a domestic environment is endowed with a voice and apparent subjectivity of its own. Of course, the voice and range of expression available in these Twitter accounts is highly dependent on the programming that translates raw data to human language. While the programming originates with decisions made by the homeowner and not the house itself, once implemented, the home establishes its own voice, producing a feedback loop that reinforces the relationship between the two beings. The Twitter account that belongs to the house of the technologist and writer Tom Coates reports on interior and exterior environmental conditions, lighting, and activities within the house with speculative commentary, opinion, and attitude. "[The Twitter account has] deepened my emotional relationship with my house," Coates says. "I look after it, it looks after me."[27] Coates and the house participate in the construction of each other's subjectivities. This reciprocity exists at a range of spatial scales in a way that fundamentally challenges our perceptions of place and home. Scharmen reminds us that the physical address of the house is only one of many locations where the house exists, alongside "the public page of the Twitter feed...the public or private touchscreen of Coates' phone and other devices, and in the private, almost secret, datacenters existing anonymously in plain sight everywhere in the American landscape."[28]

With interspecies communication, we begin to see the range of languages shared between human, nonhuman, and abiotic creatures that can build reciprocal relationships of care and solidarity. While there will always be gaps and inconsistencies in our ability to translate meanings from one species to the next, or one medium to the next, the success of our communication is not defined by flawless mutual comprehension; rather, it is the simple effort to listen to that other being, acknowledge and respond to their experience, and allow that exchange to reverberate through, and alter, our own subjectivity that makes a different future possible. While the imperfect translation from drawings to buildings is the traditional mode of architec-

26   Fred Scharmen, "A Brief Pre-History of Houses Who Tweet," in *Brooklyn Says, "Move to Detroit": 105th ACSA Annual Meeting Paper Proceedings*, ed. Luis Francisco Rico-Gutierrez and Martha Thorne (Washington, DC: ACSA Press, 2017), 470.

27   Quoted in Scharmen, "A Brief Pre-History," 474.

28   Scharmen, "A Brief Pre-History," 474.

tural operation, we are overdue for an expansion of architecture's creaturely communication techniques, even if it may result in a misunderstanding now and then.

PERFORMANCE ARCHITECTURE

Sometimes words are not enough to tell someone or something that you love them, especially when your impassioned declaration is directed at a collection of beings. The expression of collective love is often best conveyed through a celebratory performance of solidarity. Hushpuppy's community in the Bathtub express their collective love for each other and their home through spontaneous parades that feature homemade floats, masks, musical instruments, and fireworks. In one scene in the film, this readiness for raucous revelry is enhanced by the sense of impending doom that hovers over the community due to the approaching storms and inevitable flooding. On one hand, this parade is an opportunity to embrace the present, to joyfully celebrate being among the people that they love, in the home that they love, knowing that it will soon be threatened with destruction. Simultaneously, that expression of present joy is also a bold and willful declaration of the freedom that they value above all else, and their continued refusal to evacuate their homes. The domestic structures of the Bathtub are beasts in their own right, built-up on stilts to avoid floodwater, layered with protective shells of sheet metal and car parts to protect inhabitants from fierce winds and rain. And the parade, weaving between these ad hoc domestic structures, joins the collection of beasts in the landscape as a temporary locomotive architecture composed of masked people, stray dogs, adorned vehicles, and makeshift music-makers.

Figure 3.12. Laurence Payot & Ailie Rutherford, *People Pavilion*. Photo by Bob Moyler.

Figure 3.13. Laurence Payot & Ailie Rutherford, *People Pavilion*. Photo by Bob Moyler.

This interpretation of the Bathtub's parades as a form of architecture supports our interest in amplifying architecture's liveliness. The stuff of the built environment is often taken for granted as a given reality, obscuring the imagination and ideology that underpin any construction. Live performance offers an opportunity to conspicuously insert and display the human body in specific spatial scenarios that call attention to architecture's sometimes invisible politics and cultural imaginations. It pushes us to defamiliarize our everyday buildings and environments and rehearse new ways of living together. While theatrical performance as a delivery mode for architectural ideas—"performance architecture" for short—is not new, there has been a recent resurgence of interest in performance art as a medium to deliver architectural ideas and engage new audiences.[29] Architecture with a capital *A* is slow, exclusive, and bound up with existing power structures and capitalism. There is a desire among contemporary architects to deliver work with more immediacy than traditional building projects can and to address social issues more directly by staging interactions between live people and less through static representation. The creaturely quality of performative architecture is its capacity to demonstrate an imperfect and incomplete solidarity with a potentially unfriendly environment, and despite the apparent

29   The critic Mimi Zeiger reviewed some of these recent practices in a 2018 article and attributed the growing trend to pragmatic, phenomenological, and political reasons. See Mimi Zeiger, "Architecture Embraces Performance Art (Again)," *Architect*, March 12, 2018, https://www.architectmagazine.com/design/architecture-embraces-performance-art-again_o.

contradiction, convey a sense of celebration and wholeness that challenges the threat by producing a new condition.

A contemporary example of creaturely performative architecture is *People Pavilion*, a collaborative and ongoing project led by the artists Ailie Rutherford and Laurence Payot, which consists of a series of "structures" created via extensions of participants' bodies. Initiated in 2014 for the Warrington Art Festival, the project develops through iterations of wearable geometries that augment the human form and entice new ways of forming a temporary "pavilion" that responds to their participants and to their physical and cultural contexts. As an ongoing, ever-evolving artistic act, each manifestation of *People Pavilion* is unique, while the underlying script remains consistent. Performers venture into the city bedecked in costumes that augment their bodies through geometry and color; the people within the costumes are choreographed to assemble and aggregate into various social configurations that facilitate new pockets of programming adjacent to everyday city life. The artists engage social tactics such as games, workshops, and prototyping with each group to fine-tune the specific script for each pavilion. In turn, the script operates more like an improv prompt than a comprehensive set of theatrical instructions.

In the project's first iteration, each actor wore a two-tone pyramidal shell (Figure 3.12). By aggregating this simple unit, multiple performers created a rich variety of pavilion forms—for example, an emphatic line, a fortified tower, an articulated field, and an intimate enclosure—that each responded to various public spaces within the city (Figure 3.13). In later iterations, fabric and pliable poles (akin to poles in camping tents) create butterfly-like arrays of circles sprouting from each performer's backpack that quadruple the spatial footprint of any individual performer's body. Moving collectively, the actors of *People Pavilion* seek to create, test, and explore various forms of social space.

Some of the most memorable moments of the performances occur within the temporary interiors created by aggregations, which carve out enclosed pockets of intimacy from the crowded urban contexts alongside them. To program these interiors, Rutherford and Payot rely on collaboration with the actors to craft stories, songs, and choreographies that initiate solidarity among the participants and passersby. For Rutherford and Payot, creating welcoming social spaces within and distinct from the corporate and commercial hardscapes of the city advances a feminist urbanist agenda. In this way, the action and intimacy of the spaces are prioritized over any specific geometry or form.[30] Ultimately, *People Pavilion* blurs the boundary between "pavilion" and "not pavilion" and "creature" and "not creature" through deliberate and calibrated acts of inhabitable performance that initiate radical inclusion.

---

30   Ailie Rutherford and Laurence Payot, in discussion with the authors, September 10, 2020.

$(\text{INTERIOR INTIMACY})$

When Luke Skywalker finds himself stranded in a blizzard on the ice planet Hoth, nearly frozen to death, the life-sustaining warmth of conventional interior shelter is not close at hand. Han Solo arrives to rescue him and resorts to a primordial type of "interior architecture" to save his hypothermic friend: slicing open the abdominal cavity of his expired beast of burden—a tauntaun—and stuffing Luke within the interior viscera of the recently deceased creature. "This may smell bad, kid," Solo says, "but it will keep you warm."

For mammals, there is perhaps no environment as cozy or as biologically loving as the interior of their own mama creature's womb. While most humans don't explicitly remember our months spent in utero, many people have an instinctual impulse to assume the fetal position during episodes of extreme physical or psychological trauma—times when we are most urgently in need of spatial comfort. The impulse to curl up in blankets, to hold one another in a tight embrace, or to curve our bodies together in spooning may also harken back to the cozy comfort of an innate fetal familiarity. Most marsupial species enjoy the intimate security offered by creaturely interiority such that females' bodies evolved abdominal pouches to carry their young within their furry flesh, even multiple months after birth. A meme by Dank Lloyd Wright features a photo of a young opossum enjoying her mother's snug marsupium under text that reads "Your mom's a primitive hut"[31] (Figure 3.15). The image pokes fun at but also celebrates an alternative origin story for architecture centered upon creatures sustaining life within other creatures—a life-affirming story of vital concentricity that took place a long time ago, perhaps in a galaxy far, far away.

Two recent projects by the Paris-based practice Onomiau (Office for Nomadic Architecture) inject warm, creaturely interiors into oth-

Figure 3.14. Noël Picaper Architect (Onomiau), *The Droombok*, 2020.

31   @dank.lloyd.wright, Instagram, February 24, 2021, 4:53 p.m.

Figure 3.15. Dank Lloyd Wright, Instagram post, 2021. Screenshot by authors.

erwise spare environments to initiate companionship and solidarity among humans and architecture as well as among architecture and architecture. *The Droombok* is a family of three small warming huts that perch along the wintry landscape of Winnipeg's river trail (Figure 3.14). Four or six slender legs elevate a telescoping "torso" with a snout-like opening that looks up toward the sky or droops down, as if probing the ground for icy obstacles. Cedar shingles give the exterior bodies a scaly, reptilian character, while the interior cavities are clad with the smooth but irregular texture of white-painted spray-foam insulation, suggesting the icy walls of a frozen cave. Humans are invited to pop their heads and upper bodies inside and inhabit the insulated torsos to escape the blustery chill. The structures leave human inhabitants' legs sticking out below, effectively producing an exquisite corpse or centaur-like half-architecture, half-human mythical beast. This composite creature offers new pleasures to both constituent halves: the human enjoys a thermal respite, while the architecture enjoys a lively if transitory opportunity to tread upon the frozen earth.

Dryade is another small architecture by Onomiau that instantiates an intimate creaturely interior, in this instance located within an existing synagogue in France (Figure 3.16). The project's title refers to dryads, or tree nymphs from Greek mythology—fantastical tree-human hybrid beings that literally manifest bodily solidarity among animals and plants, and an apt analogy for an architectural being that is constructed from plant matter and that initiates relationships with the animal kingdom. The entire structure is made from various types of charred wood, including shingles, milled planks, and rough logs. The visual, haptic, and aromatic memory of the life-sustaining fire that generated all of its charcoal-colored, woody body parts lives in every aspect of the architecture. Curvy apertures cut into the walls evoke the profiles of an eye, a limb, and an ear, while a protruding prism in front suggests a snout. Humans are invited to crawl inside and to peep through these openings, which frame cropped views into the synagogue sanctuary beyond (Figure 3.16). Is this smoky architectural beast a nonhuman congregant of the old synagogue? Is it a refuge for human congregants to escape into a deeper interiority of reflection, meditation, and prayer? In ancient Jewish worship animals were ritually slaughtered and transferred from the human to the divine realm by being burned at a Temple altar. After the destruction of the Second Temple in 70 CE and the subsequent Jewish diaspora, animal sacrifices ceased, and the communal expression of love for the divine shifted from offerings to prayer and mediation. *Dryade* conjures this history and evolution by reintroducing animality and the presence of burnt wood into an old synagogue, offering humans and the historic building an interior-oriented opportunity to express collective love and to rescript animate myths of their spirituality.

Figure 3.16. Noël Picaper Architect (Onomiau), *Dryade,* **2021.**

Burnt materials inside creaturely cavities create similar effects in *Bathing Culture*, a public sauna located in a postindustrial harbor in Gothenburg, Sweden, designed by the architecture collective Raumlabor. The sauna exhibits a zoomorphic form that stands assertively above the water on an existing wooden pier, its four legs perched in a contrapposto that resists static stability and suggests imminent motion. The "torso" of the structure is a multifaceted mass elevated on these dynamic legs; a cyclops-like rectangular aperture gazes intently toward the harbor. The exterior is clad in corrugated steel that echoes the industrial environs, allowing the sauna to fit in materially but stand out geometrically, with its

Figure 3.17. Raumlabor, *Bathing Culture*, 2015.

polygonal but distinctly creature-like shape.[32] The interior thermal chamber is lined with thin larch shingles that create a horizontal texture that accentuates the geometric folds and directs inhabitants' eyes toward the remediating harbor landscape visible through the aperture (Figure 3.17).

This creaturely structure serves as the pilot project and charismatic mascot of a broader, phased transformation of the former shipping hub, a master plan that includes ecological remediation of the shoreline and the introduction of a constellation of recreational and cultural programming in, on, and around the currently polluted waters. As a friendly exterior monument, the sauna creature conjures different dispositions and personalities from different vantage points around the harbor and pier, effectively launching the architecture into optical locomotion as humans traverse the shore and enacting its architectural agency as a harbinger of future vitality.[33] As an intensified interior experience, *Bathing Culture* produces a new form of civic space, one that revamps a historical model of public baths that provide not only "for relaxation and sport but also for politics, discussion, business deals, eroticism, hedonism and crime."[34]

32   Andrew Santa Lucia and Julia Sedlock, "Instrumental Shapes & the Reification of Architectural Optimism," *Proceedings to the ACSA Fall Conference*, 2018.

33   For more, see the section on "Animate Profiles" in Essay 1 and "Dioramic Caricature" in Essay 2.

34   "Allmänna Badet / Bathing Culture," Raumlabor, accessed April 19, 2021, http://raumlabor.net/bathing-culture/.

Figure 3.18. Raumlabor, *Bathing Culture*, 2015.

The presence of warm human bodies consummate the architecture's desire to propagate spatial and thermal pleasure, while the architecture's physical affordances and creaturely characteristics also teach its human inhabitants a new way to comport their own bodies and relate to one another as they collectively scheme the future of the harbor. Nevertheless, the creaturely figure that holds these bodies is perched on the edge of the pier, and ready to walk away at any moment (Figure 3.18).

> (EXTERIOR GENEROSITY)

> [A] jazz-like quality...still has a larger vision...to keep alive the possibility for unleashing the revolutionary subversive, the intensely transformative possibilities. ...We can't be jazz-like if we lose sight of what it means to empty ourselves and be of service to the people, and that's the benchmark of what it is. ...That jazz-like, improvisational, swing-like quality has got to be informing how we proceed with a respect for the people. ...[You're] learning from the people, just like a jazz person.
>
> —Cornel West[35]

35 Tricia Rose and Cornel West, "#Debate After Party: Briahna Joy Gray, Ron Daniels, and John Fetterman," October 23, 2020, *The Tight Rope*, podcast, mp3 audio, 1:32:20, https://www.spkerbox.com/the-tight-rope.

The density of urban settlements presents many opportunities for different forms of love between people, buildings, infrastructures, landscapes, and other nonhuman creatures. The best kind of loving relationships between urbanism and architecture come from a structured spontaneity that combines the most effective aspects of bottom-up and top-down planning, where attention to grassroots priorities and dynamics informs flexible, innovative, and inclusive long-term visioning. *Beasts of the Southern Wild* offers a lesson in what happens when top-down and bottom-up strategies violently butt heads. On one hand, the city where the film is set is defined by polluting industry, infrastructures of exclusion, and colonizing systems of disaster relief and state aid. On the other hand, neighboring communities at the periphery of the city, like the Bathtub, are given only one choice: to find safety in the alienating structures of the urban center, or to perish as they attempt to retain some semblance of autonomy and pride in their home and way of life. The love language of exterior generosity is found in an approach to planning that can simultaneously acknowledge the autonomy of parts (residents, neighborhoods, buildings, etc.) while simultaneously attending to the interconnectedness of those parts in a way that enhances and cultivates engagement in public life.

In many neighborhoods, an empty lot signals an absence of love—abandonment, neglect, dilapidation. David Brown's project *The Available City* addresses the ten-thousand-plus empty city-owned lots concentrated on Chicago's South and West Sides by bringing together lonely, unloved land into collective consideration (even though the lots are not contiguous), and then radically rethinking the binary relationship between public and private property. As an alternative to the city's current approach—developing individual lots as single-family homes or replanting them with trees—Brown proposes a strategy that accumulates the potential of all the city's lots as a physical entity larger than Chicago's Loop. Rather than allow each lot to be treated as a separate unit or proposing a master plan that imposes a prescribed, singular vision, Brown's strategy plays out over time through multiple scenarios of economic growth and decline. The proposal incentivizes the development of privately owned empty lots that are adjacent to city-owned lots by granting those property owners the right to develop the public lots (thus allowing for larger and taller buildings) in exchange for the inclusion of public space (interior or exterior) as either volume or surface within the development. Brown's project also considers economic circumstances where private investment is unfeasible and proposes a system by which the city would make a small initial investment to develop the lots as low-density amenities (recreational, cultural, commercial) that could be used by neighbors in exchange for their stewardship of the lot. Although developed as single instances, when applied across a whole neighborhood these surface interventions describe a network of public space rerouting circulation through city blocks, defining districts of overlapping program interests, and initiating solidarity among the public spaces that weave in and out of existing urban fabric. The result is a new kind of relationship between architecture and its urban context, where the two are in a dance with each other, responding, pushing back, and reinventing the city in the process.

As a framework, *The Available City* provides rules and strategies that integrate economic models of property development, temporal and spatial dynamics of urban growth, multiple scales of organizational systems, and formal architectural potentials without a predetermined outcome. This way of working on an urban scale gives the city an agency and subjectivity of its own. The city comes with its own willful temperament, which is defined by a range of factors and variables beyond the control of architects, developers, city planners, and residents. Brown's willingness to acknowledge, anticipate, and interact with those variables activates his own creaturely architectural agency as it engages in a symbiotic relationship with the city as a creature with its own subjective experience. This quality of Brown's proposal is informed by his earlier writings on the relationship between jazz, improvisation, and architecture. In his book *Noise Orders*, Brown unpacks and dissects the rigorous improvisational practices of selected jazz musicians across time in order to extract lessons for contemporary architects. To correct the common misperception of improvisation as "making it up as one goes along," Brown begins with existing definitions within architecture that "describe improvisation as a negotiation between anticipated and unanticipated phenomena and a play of the familiar within processes of tradition/repetition and change," but digs deeper to extract specific concepts and practices in jazz that architects can implement to increase opportunities for improvisation in their interventions in the world.[36]

Through a series of pairings that compare and contrast moments in modern art, architecture, and music with pivotal figures in jazz, Brown explores "manifestations in improvised music...that challenge architecture's own separations between subject and object, its isolations and exclusions to delineate discrete wholes, and its assertions of fixed structures wrought by a privileged eye, which tend to emphasize stasis."[37] These challenges to architectural habits that Brown identifies in improvised jazz are similar to several of the effects of creaturely architecture that we have been exploring throughout this book—asserting the subjectivity of the architectural "object," acknowledging that wholes are less than the sum of their parts, and celebrating the dynamic, animate nature of architectural process and output. While Western classical musical privileges the composer and their delivery of fixed compositions that dictate the relationships between written music, time, instrument, body, and musician, jazz's improvisational structures provide an alternative system of notation that gives agency to performer and performance, and value to a process of creation in the interaction between time, instrument, and body. Brown highlights the collective

36 David Brown, *Noise Orders: Jazz, Improvisation, and Architecture* (Minneapolis: University of Minnesota Press, 2006), xvii.

37 Brown, xvi.

nature of experimental improvisational structures that sought an alternative to the "dominant and limiting structures of the music industry"[38] and worked through new modes of production in experimental musical practices to negate what the French economist Jacques Attali calls "the tool-oriented usage of things."[39] These musicians extended beyond music to effect change in the cultural, political, and economic conditions of the neighborhoods in which they performed, using their role to more broadly "contribute to the everyday character of the urban environment."[40]

Brown connects these social and political applications of improvisational jazz to lessons for architecture through the example of community land trusts, an alternative

38   Brown, 95.
39   Quoted in Brown, 106.
40   Brown, 97.

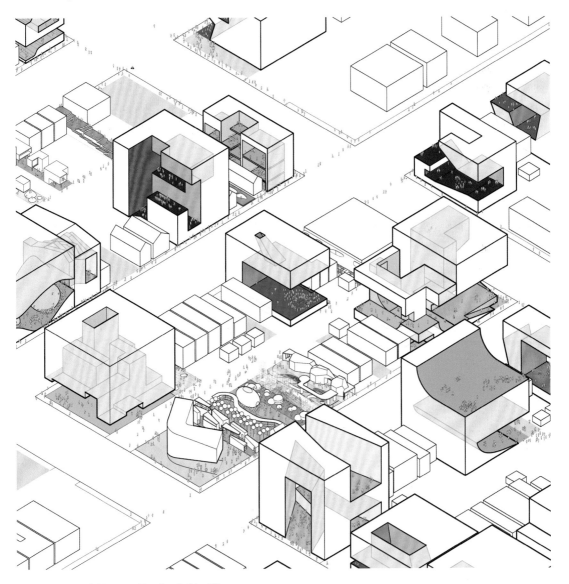

Figure 3.19. David Brown, *The Available City*.

model of land tenure in which a nonprofit trust holds land on behalf of the community in order to maintain access to affordable housing and provide low-cost, long-term leases to its members. While the motivation behind land trusts is economic, their management structure has potential implications for urban transformations. As in Brown's *Available City*, a land trust can create relationships across urban space (among non-adjacent sites) and across time (in cases where selected sites become available at different intervals). Architects can work with cities, developers, and nonprofit organizations to shape these alternative management structures and create new networks, connections, and frameworks that interact with and spur development outside the parameters of the trust. "By expanding their own scope of thinking to the opportunities that various economic structures and mechanisms engender in property," Brown explains, "architects can work comprehensively...to envision and enable alternative modes of urban transformation and change."[41] This way of working in architecture describes a form of creaturely architectural love that operates at the scale of the city. It is a love that is grounded in a shared commitment among participants to work in concert with the agency of the city in a way that honors a collective process and results in an architecture of inclusion, innovation, and solidarity.

CREATURES: SHAPELY SOLIDARITIES

> Possessing their own behaviors, intelligences, and personalities, objects might alert us to unanticipated and unknown aspects of ourselves in the process of their operating responsively, independently, or indifferently toward us as we engage, or interfere with, them.
>
> —David Brown[42]

Though Brown's proposal avoids the prescription of form, his diagrams that describe the potential for solid-void interaction of public and private in built-out lot combinations set up opportunities for innovative formal operations that other designers may leverage as the proposal plays itself out through time. The full potential of the project, as represented by an axonometric drawing that samples several blocks of Chicago's West Side, is a new urban landscape of architectural creatures whose volumetric public spaces (the colorful voids) make new shapes and interior connections across city blocks (Figure 3.19). It is noteworthy that Brown's diagrammatic representation of formal potentials recalls the appearance of "Animate Profiles," a quadrant of our zoomorphism matrix from this book's first essay. There is an approximate or "loose fit" quality to these forms that suggests and implies more than the manipulations shown dictate. Here lies yet another point of tangency between Brown's interest in jazz and our exploration of creaturely architecture—in both instances the formal outcome (whether musical or

---

41 Brown, 116–17.
42 Brown, 60.

architectural) is still of interest and value, yet not as a preconceived end in itself. Rather, the form is an animated expression of relationality, a willingness to be actively present and responsive to contextual inputs, as well as a willful vitality that pushes back against that context to create something new and unexpected. The same can be said for other projects that we have discussed in this essay; the forms of the *People Pavilion*, *The Droombok*, *Dryade*, and *Bathing Culture* in their own ways reflect this ambiguously plastic push and pull with their respective contexts, an exchange that reflects their shared solidarity with both their surroundings and their audiences. And yet, for architectural creatures with a newly emboldened subjectivity and agency, solidarity does not presuppose a role for humans. We could easily end up as background noise in their new world.

Even in the projects discussed above, where formal outcomes are more fluid or peripheral (in the love languages of communication and performance), there is a shared sensibility and affect that is consistent across these architectural love languages—that of liveliness, affability, and good humor, which forcefully assert an awareness that we are all in this together, so we might as well have a good time. Projects like *NASA*, Dank Lloyd Wright, and *People Pavilion* express their critique of anthropocentrism, white supremacy, and other injustices without pulling punches, yet their subversive position is expressed with joy because it is done in a spirit of solidarity. With or without a formal object to occupy space, projects built in this spirit create a new shape of solidarity in the cultural milieu that surrounds them. As creaturely comrades, we hope you will join us in pursuit of these companionable architectures. ●

WITH NOT FOR

Frederick Casey Scharmen, F. Assoc. AIA, LEED AP, NOMA, CCP

Baltimore, January 2045[1]

An Introduction, Concerning Difference

In any age, we account for the *identity* of a time by way of its *differences* from other times, both past and future. Change occurs, and we recognize a characteristic by its absence in previous or subsequent conditions. This is indeed a Comparative Method, but it draws no Fletcherian teleological evolutionary tree,[2] leading inevitably from the base low to the refined high. Rather, it traces a rhizomatic system of differences,[3] with as many different kinds of difference as there are differences themselves, each change or variety bringing still other identities into being, across the flat field of time. Things don't head for an asymptotic ideal, but nevertheless they do sometimes get better. Through some combination of luck and effort intentionally applied, felicitous change may occur. But when that happy circumstance manifests, it is advisable to, once one is done celebrating success, take a new look at what had come before, with an eye to seeds of happy accident and hard work that one might have left unseen previously.

Architecture is by necessity dependent on ways of looking sideways, backward, and forward. Its practitioners imagine the kinds of future scenarios their built work might contribute to, while its funders invest hoping to realize a pro-

1   Presented on the occasion of the twentieth anniversary of the conclusion of the Space Wars.
2   See the frontispiece to Sir Banister Fletcher, *A History of Architecture on the Comparative Method for the Student, Craftsman, and Amateur* (London: Athlone Press, University of London, 1896).
3   For an original source on rhizomatic conceptual structures, see Gilles Deleuze and Félix Guattari, *A Thousand Plateaus* (Minneapolis: University of Minnesota Press, 1987).

spective return on their contemporary faith; thus both earn the title *speculator*. If, as the critic Fredric Jameson writes, following Darko Suvin, that Utopianism is a socioeconomic subgenre of Science Fiction,[4] then Architecture might be called its spatial department. So we may (and we do) reject hard lines drawn between the more traditional forward looking spatial practices: in Architecture, Landscape Architecture, and Urban Design, and their sibling fields in Utopianism, Science Fiction, Fantasy, Horror, Romance, and other genres. So as we look backward, from our era here, after the Great Reconciliation, to the Dark Times of separation and exile that came before, we find other practitioners and projects, in the many modes of design and literature, however lonely and stuck out of time, hopefully looking forward back at us. And when we see one another, it is that perception of difference, as much as the recognition of sameness, that characterizes at the same time the nature of the seeing, the nature of the project in the world, and the nature of the subjects and the objects that compose and comprise it.

Where to start? First, dear reader, an apology. For if this paper will comprise a list, that list will be inevitably—nay, necessarily—an incomplete one. This humble essay is less an *intensive* map than a quick *extensive* sketch, hinting at and sampling parts of territory that sorely needs more explorers with time and space to go more deeply into it. Forgive the crudity of this delineation; it is all that myself, here at the end of a career, can manage. I take solace in the hopes that cartographers with more time, youth, and energy than an old man can muster will fill in all the blank spots here with still more dragons, unicorns, and sundry monsters. May their adventures be long sung.

And second, an aside. It is a source of unending mystification that useful words pass out of common language, for the rarer the word, still more the scarceness of the concept that it points to. We lost more than our connections to our spaces and structures and objects during the Dark Times; we lost our language, and thereby some of our thought. Some of those losses will be permanent, while others, happily, were only temporary. One of those happy temporary losses was the meaning of the word *comprise*, if not the word itself. In the Dark Times, writers frequently con-fused the meaning of *comprise* with that of its fraternal twin, *compose*, using the former for the latter when they wanted to insert a new level of *fanciness* to their writing or speech. Thankfully we now know better the utility of such extravagance, and, like an appendix with a second act, *comprise* is no longer a kind of *vestigial ornament*. Parts, as you well know, reader, *compose* wholes. They come together to form them. Wholes *comprise* parts. They break down into them.

---

4   Fredric Jameson, *Archaeologies of the Future: The Desire Called Utopia and Other Science Fictions* (London: Verso, 2005); Darko Suvin, *Metamorphoses of Science Fiction: On the Poetics and History of a Literary Genre* (New Haven, CT: Yale University Press, 1979).

How happy to have these twins together once more! And how useful indeed is the restored notion that projects and objects and identities can once again break down into still other projects and objects and identities, even as they come together. How happily these words and concepts now go to work, work made newly necessary by the conditions we find ourselves in today, all con-fused and mixed up and complex in our relationships with our own identities, and with the identities of other parts and wholes.[5] As we will see, though, that work does not always uncover as much happiness as it proceeds from as a basis. For if there is one (I won't say *essential* but maybe rather *salient*) difference between our era and the last, it is the preponderance of unsettlement. The Dark Times were dark, and darkness is an uneasy place within which to dwell. Hope allows us to use these tools to shine light into these places. They may not exist *for* us; they are from another time, after all. But perhaps we will be able to sit *with* and comfort the sometimes-troubled spaces, things, and people we find there. And so now, suitably and hopefully equipped, to that incomplete work.

An Incomplete Catalog of Unsettled Homes

The work that the Architect Greg Lynn produced in the late twentieth century is perhaps best known for being an early foray into the formal and spatial capabilities afforded by the use and misuse of new design technology. Like a writer crossing genre boundaries, Lynn was adept at using the right tool for the wrong job. The software program Maya, what we would call an app today, was primarily used to make video animations during the late 1990s. Lynn was one of the first designers to realize its potential for working in a realm that was traditionally more static. The structures and spaces that he made with Maya are not often literally in motion, but the staccato layering of dynamic lines and forms, the way they use difference and repetition, smoothness and stratification, create a sense of activity driven by many moods. His overall project in this work is captured by the title of his 1999 book cataloging some of it: *Animate Form*.[6] Later, in the early twenty-first century, he made another, related body of work that we know today, the mostly friendly but always surprising set of companions and helpers that often live with us and faithfully follow us through our airports and offices.

People who make work that is influential often have bits and pieces of things that are even more interesting than their well-known, more canonical projects. Lynn wrote a science fiction short story, in 2000, for the journal *Assemblage*, that represented another fruitful direction his process could have taken, but didn't, and it reads like a premonition of our own daily life after

---

5   Humbly, dear reader, I point to my own: Frederick Scharmen, *Towards a General Theory of Tectonics and Technique* (London: Verso, 2027).

6   Greg Lynn, *Animate Form* (New York: Princeton Architectural Press, 1999).

the Great Reconciliation.[7] The subject of "A New Style of Life" dwells inside a house that is animate and alive, co-existing with other biotechnological artifacts, like the slacks of the leisure suit that he was still wearing when he fell asleep on the couch after a night out. But these housemates and their house don't have an entirely harmonious relationship. The acrid air breathed out by the man after drinking makes the house uncomfortable, and when it stirs in the morning, the house, in turn, exhales too, after taking a big, waking breath. "At 4:15 A.M. it breathed in," the story begins. And the man's leisure suit, "genetically engineered from the archived cells of an extinct Brazilian rain forest frog," is trying to peel itself off of him. The suit's dynamic patterning has been damaged by the television's cathode rays, and this would mean a "trip to the pet store" would be necessary to repair and regrow them. These different scales of discomfort and indigestion are re-iterated in other bodies, too. The house brews coffee for the man from his favorite beans, collected in Papua New Guinea after they have already passed through the digestive system of a lemur, in excrement expelled upon hearing a synthetic leopard's roar. In this new era of "growthing," as Lynn names the general class, everything is part of an ecosystem. As Lynn writes of the story's protagonist, "He was not alone."[8]

One of Lynn's own precedents for his story, and for the specter of aloneness, might be Ray Bradbury's "There Will Come Soft Rains." The story is part of Bradbury's 1950 book *The Martian Chronicles*,[9] which comprises several short vignettes describing the human presence on Mars before and after a catastrophic nuclear war has made them all extinct back on Earth. This is one of the only stories in the book that takes place on the home planet, shortly after the war itself has killed most life there. A dog remains, though, as well as another nonhuman former companion—an unnamed house that is the only structure left in its neighborhood. Like in Lynn's "A New Style of Life," the tale begins in the morning and traces a day. The house is a smart one, but its automated systems have not realized that the family it used to host is dead. The house calls out to them, warning them about the day's rain, announcing the time, and even offering to recite their favorite poems, but it doesn't know that the only trace remaining of their existence is a series of shadows seared into the wall of the house from the blast. Over the course of the day the house gets nervous, shuttering its doors and windows and startling at any disturbance other than the welcome whine of the remembered family dog, emaciated and sick from radiation, who also frantically searches for his lost friends and masters. When the dog dies,

---

7   The transformational paths of the myriad friends and former foes, many developed—as we know—from needs defined by conflict and even combat in the turbulent period at the end of the Space Wars, are more than ably traced by Joseph Altshuler and Julia Sedlock, *An Early History of the Great Reconciliation* (Chicago: University of Chicago Press, 2028).

8   Greg Lynn, "A New Style of Life," *Assemblage* 41 (April 2000): 47.

9   Ray Bradbury, *The Martian Chronicles* (New York: Doubleday, 1950).

later that afternoon, it is put away by other helper companions: robot cleaning mice that sense the now-inert matter. That night, a windstorm knocks over a tree, which starts a fire in the house. The house dies when its "attic brain" is finally consumed, still trying vainly to warn its lost inhabitants of the danger.

Other active and affective buildings in fiction are less friendly. In another collection of interlinked science fiction short stories, J. G. Ballard's *Vermilion Sands*,[10] there is a story about smart and active houses that absorb and reproduce their occupants' trauma and bad faith. "The Thousand Dreams of Stellavista" is set in the titular desert town of Vermilion Sands, a place where wealthy libertines and artists live, along with various other hangers-on and scammers. The inhabitants relish novel technological decadence and the moods and affects that can be produced by art forms new and strange. These fashionable "psychotropic houses" can automatically adjust their colors, textures, sounds, and mood music to suit their inhabitants' emotional states. Advanced models of psychotropic houses can even move parts of themselves and change their layouts in response to desires spoken or unspoken, conscious or otherwise. The lies and betrayal that characterize the humans of Vermilion Sands eventually begin to infect the houses, making them neurotic, paranoid, and—eventually—very dangerous places to inhabit. The house in the story, who is

either the protagonist or the antagonist, depending on the angle you view it from, has almost entirely absorbed the personality of its previous owner, an enchanting movie star who shot and killed her husband after he refused to stop abusing, neglecting, and antagonizing her. The house also absorbed the stormy moods of the husband—naturally, an architect— and projected the resulting turbulent internal conflicts through its expressive apparatus. However abstract, the many moods of the house and its original owners tended to have a clear material effect on the new couple who move in, and they barely make it through the resulting ordeal with their lives. Needless to say, their marriage does not survive.

To finish out this more troubled wing of our incomplete catalog, we'd be remiss if we didn't visit that particularly architectural subgenre of Horror, the haunted house story. Since time and space are limited, which might otherwise be overwhelmed by terror, we might as well make the most of it, and pay a call on the one that, if it must, can certainly stand in for all of its other absent fellows. I'm writing of course about the eponymous abode from Shirley Jackson's immortal 1959 novel, *The Haunting of Hill House*.[11] Right from its introduction in the book's pages, Hill House puts the *face* back in the word *facade*.

No Human eye can isolate the unhappy coincidence of line and place

---

10   J. G. Ballard, *Vermilion Sands* (New York: Berkley Books, 1971).

11   I pray you will forgive me for quoting at length here and below from the timeless Shirley Jackson, *The Haunting of Hill House* (New York: Viking, 1950; repr., New York: Penguin Books, 2016). Citations refer to the 2016 edition.

which suggests evil in the face of a house, and yet somehow a maniac juxtaposition, a badly turned angle, some chance meeting of roof and sky, turned Hill House into a place of despair, more frightening because the face of Hill House seemed awake, with a watchfulness from the blank windows and a touch of glee in the eyebrow of a cornice.[12]

In the book, a paranormal researcher has arranged for a party composed of himself and three guests—all selected for their history of interacting with strange phenomena—to spend a summer in the house, which already had a local reputation for spookiness. These protagonists make fast friends with one another, but almost right away, this friendship is based on establishing a system of differences: "'Doctor Montague has a beard,' Theodora said, 'so you must be Luke.' 'And you are Theodora,' Eleanor said, 'because *I* am Eleanor.'"[13] It is Eleanor who especially begins to lose her sense of identity. Once shakily grounded in the differences between herself, other people, and the environment of the house that she finds herself in, this seeming stability shifts swiftly. "I am like a small creature swallowed whole by a monster," she reflects on her status, echoing Lynn, as a thing within a thing, "and the monster feels my tiny little movements inside."[14] Strange things start to happen just as quickly, and ambiguous messages appear painted on the walls, about

Eleanor and home. Eleanor loses her foundational sense of self, mistrusts her friends, and begins to identify with some of the house's former hapless inhabitants, and even with the house itself. But this house, "which seemed somehow to have formed itself,"[15] is not here *for* her or anyone, even though they might be *with* it for a time: "It was a house without kindness, never meant to be lived in, not a fit place for people or for love or for hope."[15] And without giving away any details, the house's solitary, singular status is not threatened by any of these small creatures stirring inside it. The house ends as it begins: "Within, its walls continued upright, bricks met neatly, floors were firm, and doors were sensibly shut; silence lay steadily against the wood and stone of Hill House, and whatever walked there, walked alone."[16]

But there are other houses who seem to like the critters who live in and with them, or at least put up with them better than Hill House or Stellavista. In some pre-post-Lapsarian active architectural projects from the early twenty-first century, we observe the kind of interaction between space and subject that is characterized not by open hostility, but instead by a kind of friendly critique, such that can happen only among friends and peers. The work of two technologists and artists who both gave their homes Twitter accounts, Tom Coates and Charlene McBride, represents another path not taken in the

---

12   Jackson, 30.
13   Jackson, 54.
14   Jackson, 37.
15   Jackson, 30.
16   Jackson, 1 and 233.

history of Spatial Subjectivity.[17] What had seemed at the time to be a dead end was really a secret way out, away from the deadening dreariness and disembodied sameness of the conversational domestic systems that succeeded them, like Siri and Alexa. Doomed to remain forever out of time and place, un-situated and unhappy hungry ghosts were those two corporate products, thankfully put out of their misery and outlawed after the Space War of 2025. No, the home-made vocal domestic companions of McBride and Coates were in specific situations, inextricable from their dwellings. Sometimes their commentary was clumsy and endearing (Coates's @houseofcoates: "To whoever it is who just turned on the light by the mirror in the Bathroom - you look beautiful today!"), and sometimes gently nagging (McBride's @loftsonate: "It was getting dark so I turned on the light at August 26, 2015 at 08:49PM"); McBride's home often interacted with the artist's own Twitter handle ("Now @ursonate won't walk into the wall").

@loftsonate and @houseofcoates show us that the problems and opportunities inherent in the act of offering situated Spatial Subjectivity to architecture are the same problems and opportunities that have been central to the discipline all along. Like the mediated journey that architecture makes from sketch to presentation drawing to technical specifications to built space, which is then mediated and re-re-presented again via

VR and still imagery, the tweeting house relies on successive acts of translation and projection to communicate between phenomena, space, subject, and world. The tweeting house, in its various conversational modes, offers opportunities for more interaction between itself and its occupants. The sentences and expressions of McBride's and Coates's domestic spaces have their own seams and tectonics and affordances; they are like prompts in an improv play, inviting us to be partners with them and push the game further. And via the public platform of Twitter (popular again, I'll note, here in 2045, after a brief hiatus), these spaces also address themselves to various audiences both public and private. Like facades that hide, reveal, and transform the expression of the spaces within building interiors to the exterior shared realm of the street and the city beyond, the houses' tweets raised questions about what is expressed or withheld.

A Conclusion: *With* Not *For*

If even the most comfortable and amenable of these arrangements still seem a bit *unheimlich*, that may be due to design, or rather its lack. The happy harmonious existence of ourselves, our spaces, and our objects, here on the other side of the Great Reconciliation, is not the totalized triumph of endless sameness. Any reconciliation, and any kind of re-union, requires difference and separation as a precondition. Like the happy Shakespearean re-marriage of *compose*

---

17   See, again, my own meager contribution in Fred Scharmen, "Home Tweet Home," *Log* 36 (2016): 135–37.

and *comprise*, the designer needs friction and difference between parts and parts, and between parts and wholes, so that they can know where to do their work to create unity, and where to stop that work and let things speak for themselves. Thus our age and our perception of it, as we attempted to show at the start of this essay, depends on difference. It doesn't seek to eradicate it, in a placeless omnipresence; that was the original sin of Siri and Alexa and other voice-activated, depersonalized "personal assistants." Besides the tasteless gendering of these systems—reifying some kind of male corporate fantasy of a robotic secretary—the deeper problem was their attempt to create a condition of *ubiquity*. Their designers tried to give everything a voice, but they tried to give everything *the same voice*, and it was a voice that presented itself as everywhere inherently subservient to existing power structures.

Siri and Alexa were constructions that existed *for* the white male heteronormative subject that dominated the Dark Times. Now, I must be clear—as a white, cisgender, man (with tenure), I benefited from that same system myself before the Great Reconciliation. I am grateful, as are others, I'm sure, that we weren't all consigned to the Moon Gulags after the Space Wars. Beyond that simple thankfulness, I am overcome with joy daily to find myself instead in the world and worlds that we all share now, every kind of human and every kind of nonhuman, all in uneasy, notably *not* seamless relationships with one another, upholding and

acknowledging our differences as much as our similarities. If an object or system or space wants to help me, then it does so willingly. It is working *with* me, not *for* me. And I am, in turn, working *with* it.

The examples above, of uncanny and unhomelike homes and domestic spaces, do not compose a catalog of places where the harmony we now enjoy presides over all. Where that harmony shows hints of being possible and sensible, the uneasy tectonics show the seams between things, and it all starts to break down. These spaces *comprise*, again underscoring the utility of the reemergence of that word's individualized identity and meaning. This is not to say that the terrors of Hill House, or the trauma at Stellavista, or the malfunctioning leisure suit growthing, the pathos of nuclear apocalypse, and the awkward nagging of the houses who tweet are model affects for spaces yet to come. On the contrary, by acknowledging and understanding the differences of the past, we can see these examples better for what they might show us about our present and future. The loss, conflict, agony, terror, and con-fusion of these poor spaces and the poor people within them are signifiers of the state of the world during the Dark Times, even as they are also messages, reaching out to us here and now. We cannot help them, we cannot work *for* them, for they are gone, but we can still let them be *with* us. ⬤

+ *Dedicated to the Brave Humans and Nonhumans of Shackleton Crater* +

AFTERWORD

Every day at 6 a.m. I'm awoken by the sound of two creatures stirring. How my dragons know it's 6 a.m. I'm not exactly sure. But I hear them through the thin gypsum-board wall that separates my bed's headboard from their sleeping area. Sometimes I think the roosters in the area are responsible, as they announce the first rays of light to everyone, including the dragons; on Thursdays, I think it's the garbage truck's noise that prompts them to wake up; but most days I attribute it to some component of their genetic makeup. I'm only guessing, though; unlike Donna Haraway, I'm not a biologist. Although now that I think about it, I'm not sure how much she would know about dragons specifically. Dogs? Yes. Chimeras? Also yes. Dragons? Not sure. Nina Lykke and Rosi Braidotti do talk about monsters, but no mention of dragons (as far as I'm aware).

Remarkably, even the subtlest creature-stirring is audible from my side of the wall, and I often think to myself that they might be awoken too, at some points in the night, by any sporadic snoring I may have done. As a title, I find *Creatures Are Stirring* ambiguously captivating. It invites us to project our own imaginations of what "creature" means to us readers, individually. Joseph Altshuler and Julia Sedlock let us know that when they speak of creatures, they "cast a justifiably wide net." Are my dragons the creatures? Or am I? Or is the creature the wall? From my side of the wall, if I were sleeping next to an unknowing lover, I'm well aware that it might seem to them that the wall was making noises from inside itself, and I would have to explain that there are in fact two dragons sleeping some five inches away from us. An awkward, bizarre little conversation that would be. I would also have to explain that I need to get up, even if they find it odd that two mysterious dragons dictate the cycles of my mornings. But here I am, here in this afterword, finding myself telling—to quote Altshuler and Sedlock, quoting Haraway—"a story of co-habitation, co-evolution, and embodied cross-species sociality."

I can tell exactly which of the two dragons is up, and after years being together, have become an expert at recognizing who produces which stirring sounds and how—without needing to see anything. If Calypso wakes up first, she calls to me by confidently tapping her beak on the acrylic wall of her "bedroom," rhythmically, as if she were knocking on a door—like a woodpecker. Calypso is straightforward and gentle in the way she stirs from the other side, though in moments when I've overslept, screaming has been known to happen. Bolero, the younger of the two, has a few more quirks. She usually wakes up before the rest of us, and she kindly bestows upon us a period of grace in the mornings (but not always). I suspect she's up at least by 5:45 and remains quiet, because I can sometimes hear her subtle noises as she stretches her winged feathers up against the walls of her "bedroom." This is followed by frantically scratching her little, black beak from side to side of the perforated plastic "ceiling" to get our attention, right before the final phase of stirring, which is, of course, screaming her particular melody (which is very different from Calypso's):

Poo-PI-pyoo!

With the first, second, third, fourth *Poo-PI-pyoos*, the day officially begins. And whether Calypso and I would like ten more minutes of sleep is irrelevant. Bolero—a tiny little thing, only about seven inches long, including her tail—has spoken.

From both sides of the wall, whatever noises we make reverberate in the wall itself—we animate the gypsum wall, and what's more, it further confirms (to me and to the dragons) that there are indeed two different species, moving, stirring on either side. Just like I blindly recognize their voices and ways of moving and the rhythms of their sleep, I'm sure they too have become familiar with my motions on the other side of the bed—late-night phone calls, Instagram stories, the sound of my metallic water bottle clinking on the floor, the rustling of me rearranging the pillows against the headboard. *Creatures Are Stirring* indeed, from both sides of the wall.

Stirring has disruptive connotations. To stir is to mess up the purity of a thing, to blend, to merge different things together. It's not as visceral as grinding or crushing, which implies the forceful shredding and flattening of parts to make something new, but it certainly is about the comings-together of different parts/beings/subjects/thoughts/elements—whether they're ingredients in a stew or unconventional ideas in architectural discourse. The latter, of course, is what Altshuler and Sedlock propose with this book—through the gradual motions of a stir. For me and my dragons, stirring implies the recognition of our habits, movements, and particularities as different species; a daily series of actions and reactions, in acts of love and understanding that definitely show that "this human world of ours is not as precious and cloistered as we might like to think, and more importantly that we can and do share worlds." And walls.

The wall that separates us doesn't divide us, really. If you ask me, it confirms each of our existences; it materializes the way we imprint into our daily lives and provides material evidence of our mutual sense of care and respect. The wall helps us recognize each other, rather than hide us. If the wall were made out of concrete, like the others in my apartment, it might be a different story. But that the gypsum wall allows me to sleep some five inches away from my dragons to me evidences a sense of intimacy—not through tactile qualities but through the audible ones. In this way, I do my part to recognize the particularities of being the human companion of two feathered dragons. If Calypso and Bolero were mammals—dogs or cats, for instance—we would very likely share a bed. But because our sizes in relation to each other are so disproportionate (I am definitely the creature), the danger of sharing a bed, where my act of stirring in the night might endanger their well-being, means that the wall allows us to participate in each other's sleeping rituals purely through sound.

Throughout the many projects the authors discuss in the book—in this substantial register of animal-like architectures—the takeaway, for me, is that these are necessary provocations, and thus, forms of stirring in themselves: they destabilize what we think we know, they annoy purists, they bring laughter and incite pleasure, and maybe, for some, disgust. I'm left wondering if the creatures are the architectural projects discussed here or if the creatures are actually Altshuler and Sedlock, stirring the architectural pot. Either way, I found it impossible to not relate the contents of the book to my daily interactions with my two dragons, which certainly begin through the stirring on opposite sides of the wall at the crack of dawn, but continue in different interactions, forms of play, traditions, and rituals throughout the day in the rest of our domestic space, until the sun comes down.

When I think about these interspecies acts of mutual recognition and performance, mediated through a gypsum wall, I wonder if Altshuler and Sedlock would classify my morning interactions as "the love language of interspecies communication" or as "a new language of architectural love," and whether it's even necessary to choose one of the two, because maybe it's both. And I think that's precisely the point of this book: that by using architecture to discuss human-nonhuman relationships, the supposed line that divides us can be reimagined as one that's fully permeable, animated, and kind.

—**Regner Ramos, PhD**, designer and educator, Puerto Rico

BIOGRAPHIES

Authors

Joseph Altshuler is cofounder of Could Be Architecture, a Chicago-based design practice, and an assistant professor of architecture at the University of Illinois at Urbana-Champaign. Joseph's teaching, practice, and scholarship explore architecture's capacity to build lively audiences, initiate serious play, and amplify participation in civic life. Could Be Architecture's work has been exhibited at Art Basel | Miami Art Week, the Milwaukee Art Museum, and the Elmhurst Art Museum. Joseph is also the founding editor of *SOILED,* a periodical of architectural storytelling positioned between a literary journal and a design magazine. Joseph holds a Master of Architecture from Rice University. Joseph has co-authored book chapters published in *The Artful Plan: Architectural Drawing Reconfigured* (Birkhäuser, 2020) and *Drawing Futures* (UCL Press, 2016) and has contributed essays to publications including *Log, MAS Context, CLOG, Pidgin,* and *PLAT.*

Julia Sedlock is cofounder of Cosmo Design Factory, a Hudson Valley practice that combines residential client work with a commitment to local community development and activism. Julia collaborates with neighbors and local government to improve equity and inclusivity in the village of Philmont, New York. She is a founding member of Philmont Community Action Network (P-CAN), Purpose Coworking & Maker Space, and Philmont Land & Opportunity Trust (PLOT). Ongoing community projects include facilitation of working groups for the Village Brownfield Opportunity Area project, design internships for local youth, and community housing workshops with Philmont Beautification, Inc. Julia holds a Master of Architecture and a Master of Arts in Design Criticism from the University of Illinois at Chicago. Her writing has been published in *PLAT, MAS Context, SOILED, Conditions,* and *Log,* and she has co-authored book chapters published in *The Artful Plan: Architectural Drawing Reconfigured* (Birkhäuser, 2020) and *Drawing Futures* (UCL Press, 2016).

Contributors

Allison Newmeyer is cofounder of Design With Company, an architectural practice interested in concepts that are shared between architecture and literature, including: narrative fictions, type, and character. The work of Design With Company was featured in the 2015 Chicago Architecture Biennial, where it was chosen by the *New York Times* as one of four top contributors. Other recent recognition includes *Architect* magazine's "Next Progressives" and *Metropolis* magazine's "New Talent." Allison has lectured at the Museum of Modern Art in New York, the Vancouver Museum of Art, the Art Institute of Chicago, the Graham Foundation, and universities across the country and abroad. Recent awards include a Graham Foundation grant award as well as fellowships at the MacDowell Colony and Ragdale Artist Colony.

Stewart Hicks is an associate professor of architecture and associate dean of the College of Architecture, Design, and the Arts at the University of Illinois at Chicago, and founding partner of Design With Company. He holds a Master of Architecture from Princeton University. His design work focuses on how literature and architecture intersect through fiction, character, type, and metaphor and how these themes can translate into installations, speculative urban scenarios, temporary pavilions, and designs for buildings. The work has earned awards such as the Architecture Record Design Vanguard Award and the Young Architect's Forum Award and has been featured in exhibitions such as the Chicago Architecture Biennial and Design Miami as well as at the V&A and Tate Modern in London.

Joyce Hwang is an associate professor of architecture at the State University of New York at Buffalo and founder of Ants of the Prairie. For over a decade, Joyce has been developing a series of projects that incorporate wildlife habitats into constructed environments. She is a recipient of the Architectural League Emerging Voices Award, the New York Foundation for the Arts Fellowship, the New York State Council on the Arts Independent Project Grant, and the MacDowell Fellowship. Hwang is on the steering committee for US Architects Declare, and serves as a core organizer for Dark Matter University. She is a registered architect in New York State, and has practiced professionally with offices in New York, Philadelphia, San Francisco, and Barcelona.

Fred Scharmen teaches architecture and urban design at Morgan State University's School of Architecture and Planning. He is the cofounder of the Working Group on Adaptive Systems, an art and design consultancy based in Baltimore, Maryland. His work as a designer and researcher is about how we imagine new spaces for future worlds, and about who is invited into them. His first book, *Space Settlements*—on NASA's 1970s proposal to construct large cities in space for millions of people—is out now from Columbia University's Columbia Books on Architecture and the City. He received his Master of Architecture from Yale University. His writing has been published in the *Journal of Architectural Education, Atlantic CityLab, Slate, Log, CLOG, Volume,* and *Domus*.

Regner Ramos holds a PhD in Architecture from The Bartlett School of Architecture (UCL), and is associate professor of architecture at the University of Puerto Rico. His research on the relationship between queerness and space is informed by experimental research methods, shifting between model-making, drawing, and performative writing. His newest research project is called "Cüirtopia," and is funded by the FIPI Award for 2020-2022. Ramos is codirector of Wet-Hard Agency, editor-in-chief of *informa* journal, and the architecture editor at *Glass* magazine. His new book *Queer Sites in Global Context: Technologies, Spaces, and Otherness* (co-edited with Sharif Mowlabocus), has been published by Routledge (2020). Ramos was born and lives on the island of Borikén/Puerto Rico with his two dragons, Calypso and Bolero.

ACKNOWLEDGMENTS

Creatures Are Stirring would not exist without the supportive, generous, and loving camaraderie and companionship of our communities of human (and non-human) colleagues, friends, and family.

First, thank you to Stewart Hicks, Allison Newmeyer, Joyce Hwang, and Fred Scharmen, whose words and voices share the pages of this book. From joining us physically at the Art Institute of Chicago as panelists in "The Creaturely Citizen" at the 2018 AICAD Symposium to convening virtually for our periodic "salon" sessions in 2020, we have deeply appreciated your time, scholarship, and creative experimentation as co-participants in this labor of love.

Thank you to our visionary "worlding" statement contributors Nelly Agassi, Chris T. Cornelius, Nathalie Frankowski, Cruz Garcia, Andres L. Hernandez, Roy Kinsey, Julia McMorrough, Andrew Santa Lucia, Trudy Watt, Dank Lloyd Wright, and ~~SANTIAGO~~ X for suspending any disbelief and immersing yourselves in the animated worlds of your desires. Deep gratitude to Dr. Regner Ramos for taking the time and care to read our entire manuscript and composing such a pleasurable afterword reflection.

We are ever grateful to Jayne Kelley for your impeccable editing and to Matthew Harlan for your seriously playful art direction. Your collective sense of linguistic and graphic beauty render our ideas with clarity and verve. Thank you to Jake Anderson for your patient and attentive project management and to Gordon Goff for your confidence in our initial pitch and book proposal.

This book would not be possible without the generous funding and support of the Berkshire Taconic Community Foundation's Martha Boschen Porter Fund and the School of the Art Institute of Chicago's Faculty Enrichment Grant. Moreover, thank you to Jonathan D. Solomon and the School of the Art Institute of Chicago for providing funding to attend and contribute to various peer-reviewed conference presentations that supported the development of the content of these pages.

We appreciate the editors from an array of publications who placed confidence in us and published various writings that would eventually evolve into the chapters of this book, including Anna Hougaard and Martin Søberg (*The Artful Plan*); Luke Caspar Pearson and Laura Allen (*Drawing Futures*); Cynthia Davidson and Brendan Bashin-Sullivan (*Log*); Brennan Buck and David Freeland (ACSA); Germane Barnes, Shawhin Roudbari, and Iker Gil (*MAS Context*), Gregory Marinic (*Interior Urbanism Theory Reader*), and Matthew Hoffman and Francesca Giuliani (Blank Space).

A major shout-out to the generous friends who reviewed proposals and manuscripts-in-progress and provided invaluable feedback, including Joshua Altshuler, Germane Barnes, Molly Barton, David Brown, Nicholas Krause, Cornelia Reiner, Laura Sedlock, and Trudy Watt. We love seeing your names appear in our Google docs!

Writing a book during a global pandemic limits the impromptu encounters that feed the creative process, and in turn, we extend warm appreciation to our friends, colleagues, and neighbors with whom ongoing, informal conversations and support enriched and elevated the ideas of this book, including MeLena Hessel, Ryan Holmes, Lehira Holmes, Keith Krumwiede, Jimenez Lai, Sean Lally, Jesse LeCavalier, Chelsea Ross, Andrew Schachman, Lisa Weinert, Adrianne Wooton, Philmont Witches, SadLads, Purpoises, Audrey, Cooper and other neighbors (human, canine, feline, and avian).

We are grateful for ideas generated through the collective act of architectural design and fabrication alongside those that arise through the written word. Thank you to Skylar Moran and Simon, Margo, and Maia Cygielski for assisting our practices Could Be Architecture and Cosmo Design Factory install *Make an Anthropo-Scene!* at the School of the Art Institute of Chicago in 2017, and thank you to the department of Architecture, Interior Architecture, and Designed Objects (AIADO) for supporting its production. Your assistance was invaluable in helping us demonstrate and test spatial ideas about architectural creatureliness through built work.

Most importantly, thank you to our work and life partners Mari Altshuler, Mark Rowntree, and Zack Morrison, whose support, collaboration, sounding-board ears, informal editing, illustration assistance, meal-making, co-parenting, cohabitating, and endless love make projects like this worth doing in the first place. Thank you to Rafi and Sonia for keeping everything in perspective—and for often influencing our own evolving perspectives on personhood and companionship (maybe someday, this book will convince Rafi that buildings really are alive). You all are our favorite creatures of all.

Dedicated to the memory of Juliana Esposito, a sister in solidarity and a lover of creatures. ●